Aircraft Wrecks of the Pacific Northwest

Volume 3

David L. McCurry

With Cye Laramie

Hoosick Falls, New York
2017

First Edition published in 2017 by the Merriam Press

First Edition

Copyright © 2017 by David L. McCurry
Book design by Ray Merriam
Additional material copyright of named contributors.

All rights reserved.
No part of this book may be used or reproduced in any manner whatsoever without written permission, except in the case of brief quotations embodied in critical articles or reviews.

WARNING
The unauthorized reproduction or distribution of this copyrighted work is illegal. Criminal copyright infringement, including infringement without monetary gain, is investigated by the FBI and is punishable by up to five years in federal prison and a fine of $250,000.

The views expressed are solely those of the author.

ISBN 9781576386217
Library of Congress Control Number: 2017937972
Merriam Press #AH11-P

This work was designed, produced, and published in
the United States of America by the

Merriam Press
489 South Street
Hoosick Falls NY 12090

E-mail: ray@merriam-press.com
Web site: merriam-press.com

The Merriam Press publishes new manuscripts on historical subjects, especially military history and with an emphasis on World War II, as well as reprinting previously published works, including reports, documents, manuals, articles and other materials on historical topics.

Table of Contents

Introduction and Acknowledgements 5
Chapter 1: Grand Coulee P-63A Kingcobra 9
Chapter 2: Feathered Engine: A B-24's Failed Go Around 15
Chapter 3: "Tommy's Tigator" 21
Chapter 4: United Flight 173: Portland Oregon 28
Chapter 5: Missing F4F Wildcats Found 43
Chapter 6: Mid-Air Over The Olympics 50
Chapter 7: General Aviation and Unidentified Sites 54
Chapter 8: "Dutch Roll" Sheds Engines From Boeing 707 Jetliner 60
Chapter 9: "Firewood One" 68
Chapter 10: B-47E Refueling Technique Turns Night Mission Into Disaster 73
Chapter 11: "Article 123": The Cover Up 82
Chapter 12: Speed Brakes: A Fatal Consequence to a Sabre Jet Forced Landing 88
Chapter 13: High Altitude Stall Downs P-47D Thunderbolt 95
Chapter 14: Controlled Flight Into Terrain 101
Chapter 15: Failure of Engine Turbine Wheel Severs Aft Fuselage from F-86D Sabre .. 109
Chapter 16: Mid-Air Break-Up: The Touchet B-24 Tragedy 116
Chapter 17: Broken Connecting Rod Ends Airacobra Night Flight 124
Chapter 18: The Salish Peak F-89s 131
Chapter 19: Ejection From F-86 Sabre Jet Conforms With Fire Warning Light 137
Chapter 20: Echelon Formation Creates Airacobra Collision 142
Chapter 21: Blackbird's Night Training Mission Goes Awry 148
Chapter 22: Mystery Solved: Super Sabre Found Hundreds Of Miles Off Course 154
Chapter 23: Inclement Weather: A Trap for a Vultee BT-13 163
Chapter 24: Snow Storm Dooms B-25 On Mt. Timpanogos 168
Chapter 25: Phantom Jet Disappears On Routine Training Mission 174
Chapter 26: Regina Airlines DC-3: Attempt at VFR Flight Proves Fatal 180
Chapter 27: The Dakota Crewmen of Sulphur Mountain 185
Chapter 28: In Weather Over Mountains And Out Of Gas 195
Appendix I: Washington State Crash Locator List 203
Appendix II: Oregon Crash Locator List 206
Appendix III: Idaho Crash Locator List 207
Bibliography and Suggested Reading 208

Dedication

I would like to dedicate this book to the Project Remembrance Team whose members located throughout the United States are dedicated to building memorials in remembrance of our lost but not forgotten aviators.

Cover Photo

Vertical stabilizer from General Dynamics F-111A, serial number 66-042, which crashed on 12 February 1969, taking the lives of Maj. Robert E. Jobe and Maj. William D. Fuchlow. The crash site is located at 9,100 feet of elevation in the Pequop Mountain Range, 23 miles southeast of Wells, Nevada. (Photo by Dave McCurry)

Back Cover Photo

U.S. flag marks the crash site of a Navy Grumman EA-6B Prowler which crashed near Harrington, Washington, on March 11, 2013, taking the lives of Lt. Valerie C. Delaney; Lt. Cmdr. Alan A. Patterson; and Lt. William B. McIlvaine. The crew was assigned to the Tactical Electronic Warfare Squadron, VAQ-129, based at Whidbey Island NAS, Washington. (Photo by Dave McCurry)

All photos credited.

Introduction and Acknowledgements

INTRODUCTION

IN the past decade, the role of aircraft wreck hunting as a hobby has changed more toward protecting crash sites as memorials, honoring those whom were lost, bringing closure to families, and placing memorial plaques in honor of those who were lost in these tragic accidents. For those of us who are offspring from the World War Two generation, we feel an ever stronger sense of respect in honoring those that gave their lives for such a great cause. There is a strong sense of responsibility for us in keeping their names alive, and maybe it might be that we are the last real link to them?

As youngsters we witnessed the war heroes that received a lot of attention especially those involved in the flying world, but it was sad to think of the aircrews that were lost states-wide whose names were never known. They never had a chance to fight a war, but they were just as much a hero as anyone else. Just think of where they might have gone in life.

Seventy plus years ago, the losses in training were huge. Pilots and air crews were disciplined and well trained, but unfortunately expendable. Most of the crew members were between the ages of 18 and 25 years of age, and had only a very limited amount of experience. Because of the war effort, thousands of pilots were being trained during a short intense period of time, and then turned loose to fly large high-performance aircraft while having only a few hundred hours of flying experience. Imagine having a very limited amount of "instrument-type" of flying available and having to train at night, over mountains, and in inclement weather. If the pilot or navigator made a serious mistake, the entire crew may have paid the ultimate price. Becoming lost during instrument flight over mountainous terrain, and while maneuvering in weather at night in order to re-orient one's position, was a major cause of accidents, particularly in the Pacific Northwest.

There were mechanicals caused from relatively new untested equipment, but there were also safety concerns associated with low-level strafing and bombing missions, mid-air collisions from formation flying, effects from hypoxia, and the unknowns of high-speed stalls created by the development of new wing designs. Another cause of accidents was attributed to heavy underpowered multi-engine aircraft struggling to clear terrain as well as those suffering engine failures and not being able to maintain altitude. It was fairly common for individual Army Air Bases to loose four or more aircraft to training accidents per month.

Having spent most of my life serving as a professional pilot; I was very fortunate in having listened to their stories and to have flown with hundreds of former WWII pilots over a thirty year span of time. Wow do I ever miss them, and back then, it seemed like time spent flying with those aviators would never end. Most of them have passed on now, but they have left a legacy in my mind that will last forever.

With this having happened so long ago it is easy now to view an aircraft crash site as an interesting pile of bent metal, but we need to keep in mind that there were humans involved, many who may have lost their lives there. Just like an accident that may happen today; they are and were, all traumatic events that affect many lives for decades beyond.

Most of the older aircraft accidents that happened during war time were kept mostly quiet and were considered classified. Because of that, family members were notified that one of their loved ones was deceased, but not necessarily given any facts or locations on exactly where an accident had occurred, other than a general location. Today with accident reports becoming de-classified and with internet searches available, surviving family members are starting to discover groups that are sincerely involved in bringing closure to families who have spent many years wondering what had happened to their loved ones, and where their accidents had taken place. Many of these family members today are interested in visiting crash sites and building memorials where legal to do so.

One such group founded by G. Pat Macha called the Project Remembrance Team, works incredibly hard at granting the wishes of surviving family members, and making sure that the memory of their loved ones is not forgotten. Pat Macha, who has been involved in aircraft wreck hunting for over fifty years, can commonly be seen volunteering his time in taking surviving family members of crash victims on cross-country hikes to crash sites, making videos of the experiences, writing books, and involving himself in speaking engagements around the country. His kind considerate acts have made a huge mark within the wreck hunting community.

Because of our interactions involving wreck hunting groups, "Wreckchasing," which are located throughout the entire United States; I have decided to include a few wrecks that we have documented outside of the boundaries of the Pacific Northwest. We all work together on projects all over the country and know each other like family. Each spring, usually in Las Vegas, Nevada, our wreck hunting groups meet together for a week-long International Wreckchasing Symposium. During the symposium, the group normally spends two days involvement with speaking events and programs on a variety of topics involving aviation history, wreck hunting adventures, the Project Remembrance Team, early airway navigation beacons and arrows, underwater aviation archaeology, book writing, wreck hunting videos, and much more. Several days before and after the symposium are spent hiking to historical aircraft wrecks that are located within the surrounding area. Many in the group are very supportive of museum projects as well.

I have a strong admiration for those persons actively involved in Project Remembrance, and may we forever honor and respect the memory of those whom were loved and lost.

PROJECT REMEMBRANCE TEAM

The Project Remembrance Team is a volunteer organization dedicated to facilitate requests of next of kin who wish to learn more about the loss of loved ones in aircraft accidents, including crash site visitations, and the placing of memorials where legal to do so.

In the past twenty-five years the Project Remembrance Team has assisted more than one-hundred next of kin to fulfill their wishes for accident reports, maps, photographs, and crash site visitations. On one occasion where a crash site could not safely be reached on foot, a flyover was arranged. More than a dozen memorial markers have been placed at, or near crash sites, all with the permission of the property owners, be they private, state, or federal.

All missions are completed with respect and admiration for those who have come forth to honor the memory for those whom they have loved and lost. Losses suffered by our first responders, and members of our armed forces receive an appropriate extra measure of attention.

Project Remembrance founder,
and SoCal Team Leader

G. Pat Macha

ACKNOWLEDGEMENTS

I would like to sincerely thank the following people for their much appreciated hard work and contributions: Vicki McCurry; Don Hinton; G. Pat Macha,WWW.aircraftwrecks.com; Ken Potter, Oregon Wreckchasing; Judy Leonard; Richard Rice; Gary Sanders; Del White; Dale Martin; Sam Parker; Chris Baird; Dave Fish; Jim Ledbetter; NWHikers.net; Jared Swisher; Shawna Whelan Photography; Tom Townsend; Gary Vincent; Andy Dewey; Brad Metz; Boeing Aircraft Company; Ken Miller; Nick Veronico, Wreckchasing; Cye Laramie; Richard Silagi; Jim McDole; Delbert Dodd; Terry Schaeffer; Jason Watt; Craig and Rasa Fuller, AAIR; Dave Trojan; Dave Schwarz; Jeff Blackmon; John and Deb Wirt; Larry Lenz; Lauren Totusek; Lynn Gamma; Mickey Russell; and Sylvester Jackson Jr., Department of the Air Force, Air Force Historical Research Agency; Jeff Schroeder; Art Jackson; Scott Waeschle; Mike Robinson; Al Potter; Russ Burtner; Vance Burck; Scott Dickinson; Todd Busby; Joe Idoni; Ray Franco; Tony Moore, The X-hunters; Jerry Bowen; John Craycraft; Evelyn Craycraft; Joe Craycraft; Randy Williams; Warren Bowen; Mary Bowen; Cherilyn Eager; Marc McDonald; Eric Lund; Caleb McCurry; Kristy McCurry; Carole Quallio; Jeff Sprague; Frank Jongenburger; John Barone; Jim Ward; Patty Ward; and Michael Ward.

David L. McCurry
Pasco, Washington

The Project Remembrance Team is a volunteer organization dedicated to facilitate requests of next of kin who wish to learn more about the loss of loved ones in aircraft accidents, including crash site visitations, and the placing of memorial markers where legal to do so. (G. Pat Macha)

Don Hinton, an aviation historian and a major contributor to our aircraft wreck hunting adventures, checks out a North American F-100 Super Sabre crash site located near Cherry Creek, Nevada. (Photo by Dave McCurry)

G. Pat Macha, founder of the Project Remembrance Team, along with his wife Mary Jane as they visit a McDonnell Douglas F-4D Phantom II crash site north of Las Vegas, Nevada. (Photo by Dave McCurry)

Dave McCurry

Dave McCurry, author of Volumes 1-3 of Aircraft Wrecks of the Pacific Northwest, photographing a piece of wreckage at the crash site of B-52D, 56-0591, "Tommy's Tigator," located west of Burns, Oregon. (Photo by Ken Potter)

Author Dave McCurry grew up an avid outdoorsman involved in hunting, fishing, and mountain climbing, but spent the majority of his life flying fixed-wing aircraft. As a young kid in the late 1950s and early 1960s; Dave scanned the skies taking note of every type of old radial-engine aircraft that flew over knowing that someday he would be a part of the flying world. Starting out young, he had already co-owned two airplanes by the time he reached twenty-one years of age. After more than forty years involvement in flying; Dave has served as a flight instructor, contract pilot, and charter pilot, having had the opportunity to fly more than 200 different types of single and multi-engine aircraft. Having an intense interest in aviation history, he cherished the opportunity to study World War II aircraft wrecks that are located all over the Pacific Northwest. With twenty years of experience in wreck hunting and aviation archaeology; Dave was able to produce three great books detailing Aircraft Wrecks of the Pacific Northwest. Other interests include traveling to various parts of the world and actively photographing wildlife in their natural settings.

Chapter 1

Grand Coulee P-63A Kingcobra

By David L. McCurry

2ND Lieutenant Glen L. Ryland took off from the Ephrata, Army Air Force Base at 1710, 9 August 1944, in the number 4 position flying a Bell P-63A Kingcobra, serial number 42-69016, as a four-ship flight on a scheduled altitude formation and camera gunnery mission. The group, part of the Fourth Air Force, 430th AAFBU Flight Section "D" was based at the Ephrata Army Air Force Base, Ephrata, Washington.

The flight climbed to 15,000 feet of altitude heading north of Grand Coulee, Washington, and remained there for approximately five minutes, then descended to 10,000 feet while making 180 degree turns in a string formation.

The U. S. Army Air Forces Accident Report stated that Lt. Ryland had thought Flight Leader, 1st Lieutenant George D. Alber, was going to break through the clouds, so he descended down through the clouds himself. While in the clouds Lt. Ryland checked all of his instruments and all appeared normal. With everything functioning normal, he noted that his airspeed was not excessive, indicating 300 mph in a normal dive just before he broke out of the clouds. As Lt. Ryland broke out of the clouds he found himself in a steep dive, nearly vertical. Immediately he was thrown to the left side of the cockpit very violently and proceeded to get his head bumped around inside the cockpit on all sides. He remembered moving the control stick around noticing that there were no control pressures on it at all.

His being buffeted around the cockpit knocked him out and when he regained consciousness, he noticed the right door was missing. His eyes were filled with blood and he hadn't noticed that the wings and tail section had broken off from the plane. After being stunned from hitting his head real hard, Lt. Ryland unfastened his safety belt and tried to get out of the plane which took a great deal of effort. He got his head and shoulders out and kicked violently with his right leg, gashing it at the same time, which then freed him. After being freed from the stricken plane, he pulled the ripcord almost immediately and the parachute opened very violently breaking his collar bone.

As Lt. Ryland floated down for the next minute and a half, pieces of burning wreckage came down past him off to his left. He was not able to distinguish what parts they were. He landed about one-half mile from the burning fuselage which he saw as he came down, and about 100 yards from the separated wings.

After leading the flight down to skim the top of the cloud deck at about 10,000 feet, Lt. Alber pulled up and started a right turn to reform the flight which had gotten into a string formation. He only saw two other planes so he started making radio checks. Lt. Ryland didn't answer, so he flew to the edge of the cloud deck and took the other two under. Lt. Alber spotted a grass fire so he had Lt. Thomas and Lt. Shearer, flying the other two planes, hold their altitude while he descended down to investigate. As he descended; Lt. Alber spotted the demolished plane and noticed the prop and separated wings, so he called the base and gave them the information. He didn't see a parachute so he assumed that Lt. Ryland was still in the crashed plane. Lt. Alber then returned to the base where he took a Vultee BT-13 training aircraft and guided crash trucks to the crash site. On returning over the crash site, Lt. Alber found that the local fire department had already arrived on the scene.

After landing by parachute, Lt. Ryland crawled out of his harness and attempted to spread the chute out to make it more visible from the air. After that, he went back to his harness and opened up the first aid kit and took out some morphine. He was about to give himself a shot when a farmer by the name of Albert Scott pulled up in his truck and then administered the morphine shot to Ryland. Mr. Scott left Lt. Ryland there for about twenty minutes while he went and made a telephone call. Scott arrived back with a sedan, helped Ryland into the back seat along with the chute, then drove him about seven and one-half miles to the Coulee Dam Hospital where they gave him first aid and put him to bed.

ACCIDENT CAUSE

Wreckage from the P-63A aircraft was scattered over a one-mile distance. The wings were found fifteen feet apart with the fuel tanks still intact, and were found one-half mile from the fuselage. The entire tail section was found three hundred yards beyond the wings, and the right door was found half-way between the wings and tail section.

It was the opinion of the Aircraft Accident Committee that the speed of this P-63 airplane when it came out of the cloud layer was greater than 300 mph because the flight was flying at 300 mph on top of the cloud deck. For an airplane to descend through 1,000 feet of cloud and emerge in a near vertical dive would indicate a greater speed. The Committee was also of the opinion that both wings and the empennage came off shortly after the airplane came out of the clouds. Structural failure was determined to be the cause of this accident and it was recommended that the wings of the P-63 type aircraft be reinforced to prevent similar types of accidents.

P-63A KINGCOBRA SERIAL NUMBER 42-69016 CRASH SITE TODAY

While searching for another crash site in the general area; we were directed to a fellow who has had this crash site located on his own property for his entire life without him knowing too many of its details. The few details that he was aware of did lead to our discovering the identity of the site though. One item of interest that he mentioned was finding a door from the P-63 on his property years ago, but he couldn't remember what he had done with it.

The crash site of P-63A, serial number 42-69016, is located five miles north of the Grand Coulee Dam in Washington, State, on the west end of a cow pasture and scattered up the steep slope of a high hill in that area. Cows grazing in the area have disturbed the site quite a bit, but after finding a few parts of this aircraft by the use of a metal detector, it was fairly easy then to track the line of wreckage to a point where we could then follow parts up the slope.

There is not a lot left at the site today, but what we did find was easily identifiable as coming from a P-63 Kingcobra aircraft. Some of the more notable parts identified were a face plate from an oil pressure gauge, an exhaust stack from a V-1710 Allison engine, an oil strainer access door, parts from a 37mm canon, a piece of wreckage with a Bell P-63 part number on it, and part of a window frame with pieces of Plexiglas still in it. Hundreds of small mostly unidentifiable fragments of aluminum are scattered about the area as well.

The view of the crash site indicated that the fuselage of the P-63 had impacted fairly steep ground dispersing its energy mainly in one small area. The wings and tail section from the Kingcobra had been recovered during the accident investigation years ago.

Bell P-63A Kingcobra powered by a 1,325-hp Allison V-1710-93 liquid-cooled 12-cylinder piston engine had a service ceiling of 43,200 feet and a maximum speed of 409 m.p.h. Armament was one 37mm canon mounted in the nose and four fixed forward-firing .50 caliber machine-guns, two in the nose and two mounted in the wings. This example is displayed at the Yanks Air Museum in Chino, California. (Photo by Nicholas A. Veronico)

General view looking toward the east from the crash site of Lieutenant Glen L. Ryland's Bell P-63A Kingcobra, serial number 42-69016. This accident occurred on August 9, 1944, four miles north of the Grand Coulee Dam in Washington, State. (Photo by Dave McCurry)

Our hiking group as they assembled prior to tracking the crash path of the Kingcobra fighter plane uphill. (Photo by Dave McCurry)

One of the first pieces of the aircraft that had been located was this window frame with pieces of Plexiglas still in it. (Photo by Dave McCurry)

This exhaust stack from the P-63's Allison V-1710 engine was among the first items found at the crash site of 42-69016. (Photo by Don Hinton)

Our hiking group which included (from left) Don Hinton, Vicki McCurry, Richard Rice, and Judy Leonard as they proceeded up the slope looking for bits of wreckage from the crashed P-63 aircraft. (Photo by Dave McCurry)

Oil pressure gauge faceplate from Lt. Ryland's crashed P-63 was found a short way up the steep slope. (Photo by Dave McCurry)

Richard Rice and Don Hinton examine a small bit of wreckage at the P-63 crash site found by use of Don's metal detector. (Photo by Dave McCurry)

Back plate from an SCR 522 radio transmitter found at the crash site of 42-69016. This type of transceiver was used in U.S. Army aircraft to provide two way radio telephone communications between aircraft and to ground stations. (Photo by Dave McCurry)

Comparison photo shows the now and then impact area of the P-63 Kingcobra with little difference other than the once thriving tree now being a dead snag. (Photo by Don Hinton)

Oil strainer access door found at the crash site. (Photo by Dave McCurry)

Richard Rice and Don Hinton take a few minutes to ponder the trajectory of Lt. Ryland's P-63 Kingcobra before it crashed into the slope they are standing on. (Photo by Dave McCurry)

Chapter 2

Feathered Engine: A B-24's Failed Go Around

By David L. McCurry

AFTER experiencing an oil leak, pilot 2nd Lieutenant Gilbert A. Milam, flying Consolidated B-24J, serial number 42-64155, had shut down and feathered an engine prior to attempting a landing. At 1752 Pacific War Time (PWT), on this date of June 15, 1945, the B-24 Liberator bomber was returning from a local training mission to the Walla Walla Army Air Base, Walla Walla, Washington. The bomber came in fast and landed long on the halfway mark of the runway, the aircraft then bounced into the air and pilot Milam made a three-engine go around.

Liberator 42-64155 had just previously called the control tower and advised them that "the number 3 engine was feathered because of an oil leak, and the bomber was approaching for an intended emergency landing." Theodore Wodzien, the tower officer on duty, had given Lt. Milam landing instructions and Milam had acknowledged. He made a normal traffic pattern and with a high fast approach; Lt. Milam touched down way past his intended touchdown point, floating because of the high approach speed. After the successful go around and with the bomber now on the downwind leg; tower controller Wodzien advised Lt. Milam that he was too low for a three engine approach and to get some altitude. Lt. Milam acknowledged by saying "Roger." While climbing on the downwind, the tower also advised him to unfeather the number 3 engine if he had to. Again, Lt. Milam acknowledged "Roger."

Other witnesses stated that the B-24 crossed very low over the town of Walla Walla, Washington, and turned downwind, still lower than the traffic pattern altitude. Positioned on base leg, the start of a turn toward final appeared normal from observations made by the tower personnel. Upon turning final, the plane overshot the extended centerline of the runway and started to turn back in order to line up with the runway. The bank angle steepened into a 70 degree plus bank angle where the bomber stalled, made a half-turn spin, and then dove into the ground two miles north of the Walla Walla Air Base.

The B-24 bomber was totally demolished after a terrific impact, and exploded into flames killing all nine airmen aboard instantly. Fire crews arrived eight minutes after the accident had occurred and found the aircraft to be a total loss with the entire crew dead.

The crew members killed in the crash included: 2nd Lt. Gilbert W. Milam (pilot); F/O Henry B. Eging (co-pilot); F/O Harry R. Burns (navigator); Cpl. Charles J. Gianini (bombardier); Cpl. Jack S. Cassidy (engineer); Cpl. Earl L. Gross (radio operator); Cpl. Raymond G. Apodaca (gunner); Pfc. Stephen Miskevich (gunner); and Pfc. Wendell S. Jones (gunner). All were assigned to the Fourth Air Force, 423rd Army Air Forces Base Unit, Walla Walla Army Air Field, Washington.

INVESTIGATION CONCLUSIONS

A "Cardinal Rule" was that no B-24 aircraft would attempt a three-engine go around, in this case with the number 3 engine shutdown and feathered. The danger of steep turns at low altitudes, especially with the inside engine dead, had been constantly stressed on this base. Steep turns and turns into the dead engines and high speed stalls had also been an important part of all of the Emergency Procedures instruction on the base.

It was considered that the pilot of B-24J, 42-64155, could have restarted the number 3 engine long enough for a safe landing or simply circled the air base while gaining enough altitude to complete a safe landing.

As for a violation of the Fourth Air Force Memorandum 51-618, dated 9 September 1944, paragraph 6 quoted: "If any one of the following conditions exists, with one or more engines inoperative, except in an extreme emergency, the airplane commander will not pull up and go around."

On completion of the investigation, it was found that the engines and aircraft had burned beyond investigation possibilities as to the oil leak on the number 3 engine.

B-24J, 42-64155: CRASH SITE TODAY

While attending an Experimental Aircraft Association meeting in Walla Walla, Washington, during February of 2014, I was approached by a man by the name of Del White whom asked if we could provide information on a large bomber aircraft that had crashed on his family farm nearly seventy years ago. Del was only three years old at that time but could still vividly remember the aftermath and large fire caused by the crash of this bomber. Others around the area knew of this bomber crash, but no one knew exactly what type of aircraft this was and assumed that it was probably a Boeing B-17 bomber. Del asked that after his field was plowed and before planting peas, if we could meet for a day and metal detect the area where the plane had crashed. The site is located two miles northwest of the Walla Walla Regional Airport, which during World War II had been the Walla Walla Army Air Base.

Our plan was to meet with Del at his farm on April 5th, but it turned out that he had an obligation with his grandson on that day. Del then arranged for us to meet with his daughter-in-law, Amy, at the same point and time to lead us to the crash site.

After a quarter mile trek uphill to the crash site area, we immediately noticed that there was no discernable trace of a large bomber having crashed there after sixty-nine years of plowing and planting crops on this field. The only thing in view was a small red flag that Del had left, marking the spot where he had plowed up a few small parts in the past.

Using a metal detector, we immediately started getting hits on what we found to be melted aluminum slag. It was obvious that the remains of the bomber had stopped and burned there. As we moved further to the southeast, we started finding unburned internal structural parts, fuselage and wing skins, Plexiglas, 0.50 caliber ammo casings, and finally at the far end, cockpit items.

It was like the ultimate type of archaeology work in tracing where the bomber had first hit to where it came to rest and burned. You could then clearly see which direction the bomber had been moving when it crashed. We had heard varying stories of the aircraft having been aligned on final approach for a landing at Walla Walla, but now it was very obvious to us that the bomber was actually heading away from the air base after the half-turn spin when it crashed.

As we documented parts that we had found; I noticed that none of them resembled Boeing Aircraft construction. On closer examination I identified a small wing skin, cowling parts, and then part numbers starting with the number "32" identifying this as being a Consolidated B-24 bomber. What an interesting way to resolve this mystery aircraft.

Consolidated B-24 Liberator bomber in this photo would have closely resembled the B-24J, serial number 42-64156, which crashed northwest of the Walla Walla, Washington, Army Air Base on June 15, 1945. (U.S. Army Air Forces)

Using the small red flag that Del White had left in his plowed field as a guide; we immediately started metal detecting small bits of melted aluminum slag from the bomber aircraft. (Photo by Dave McCurry)

Don Hinton and Vicki McCurry finding parts from the bomber at a point where we determined the bomber had first impacted the ground. (Photo by Dave McCurry)

Photo shows some of the various items that we were starting to find. (Photo by Dave McCurry)

Some of the items included electrical parts and some sort of selector valve. (Photo by Dave McCurry)

Looking over the plowed hill we could see Del White's farm shop at the right center of the photo and his son's house on the left. (Photo by Dave McCurry)

After several hours of metal detecting the crash site of B-24J, 42-64156, we assembled a display of all of the items found. (Photo by Dave McCurry)

Some of the items that were fairly identifiable as coming from the B-24 bomber were a small cowling part, Plexiglas, fuselage skin, and wing skins. These parts are commonly identified in Consolidated Aircraft type construction. (Photo by Dave McCurry)

This part shows inspector stamps and numbers. (Photo by Dave McCurry)

An internal structural part from the B-24 bomber shows the part number beginning with the number "32" indicating this to have come from a Consolidated B-24. (Photo by Dave McCurry)

Chapter 3

"Tommy's Tigator"

By David L. McCurry

"TOMMY'S Tigator," a Boeing B-52D jet bomber, serial number 56-0591, was scheduled to conduct a test flight lower than 500 feet above the ground on an elliptical course from The Dalles, Oregon, to Malheur Lake, to Burns, Oregon, then on to Walla Walla, Washington, at near its maximum speed of 638 miles-per-hour. The Strategic Air Command (SAC) needed to know if the Stratofortress bomber (specifically designed to fly at high altitudes) could survive the secondary structural stresses caused by violent air turbulence found at very low altitudes. The flights were being conducted to determine the feasibility of flying the world's largest bomber under enemy radar warning systems to deliver a nuclear payload. It was during the height of the "Cold War" and one of the intended targets would be the Soviet Union.

At 11:05 a.m. on June 23, 1959, Tommy's Tigator took off from Boeing Field in Seattle, Washington, for the experimental low-level flight test. Five employees of the Boeing Aircraft Company which were on board the B-52 bomber conducting the test on this day included: Lewis E. Moore (commander/pilot); Joseph Q. Keller (copilot); Gerald G. Green (navigator); Charles K. McDaniel, and Neil Johnson (flight-test engineers).

The B-52D aircraft had been making test runs over eastern Washington, Oregon, and Idaho since April 10, 1959, and was loaded with special electronic equipment for measuring stresses on the airframe and flight control surfaces.

At 11:30 a.m., Tommy's Tigator radioed that it was over The Dalles and preparing to descend for the low-level test. No further transmissions were received from the pilot after it passed this checkpoint.

Witnesses working in the area reported seeing the B-52 flying at an extremely low altitude around 12:00 noon before it pitched up, burst into flames, and then crashed into the ground. Other witnesses reported seeing the bomber coming up a canyon when parts started falling off moments before the crash. Tommy's Tigator had crashed in sparsely populated high-desert country on the edge of the Ochoco National Forest in Harney County, 35 miles west of Burns, Oregon. Shortly after the accident, a logging crew working in the area surrounded the burning wreckage scattered over a wide area with six tractors, and helped control fires started by thousands of gallons of spilled jet fuel. The impact of the crash nearly disintegrated the aircraft scattering parts for approximately a mile and a half in all directions. After notifying the U.S. Forest Service, Oregon State Patrol officers and airmen from the 634th Aircraft Control and Warning Squadron at the Burns Air Force Radar Station immediately rushed to the crash site and prohibited access to all but authorized personnel. All five members of the crew were found to have perished in the accident.

AIR FORCE INVESTIGATION

The first pieces of debris found along the flight path were from the tail section, then sections of the fuselage and parts of the main wing assemblies. Further along the flight path, investigators found remains of the burned out cockpit and the eight jet engines, some found over a quarter of a mile away from the flight path.

After all of the wreckage had been identified, photographed, and mapped, the Air Force brought in heavy cranes and lifted large pieces of the aircraft onto flatbed trucks. All of the debris that had been collected was then transported to a hangar at Mountain Home AFB in Mountain Home, Idaho, for a detailed examination.

The investigation by Air Force and Boeing experts concluded that the accident was caused by the catastrophic failure of the horizontal stabilizer affecting the B-52's longitudinal stability. The plane was not designed for the excessive turbulence of high speed low-level flight, and began to disintegrate. Minus the horizontal stabilizer, the nose pitched up sharply until it stalled, then the plane impacted a knoll and exploded. There was little chance of crew survival because of the plane being at such a very low altitude; the crew had no real opportunity to eject.

Despite this tragedy, the test flight yielded a significant piece of information. The airmen monitoring the radar scopes at the Burns Air Force Radar Station were unable to detect the presence of the B-52 skimming the desert floor through a series of canyons. The tactic was effective but unquestionably risky. Boeing soon fixed the problem with the horizontal stabilizer on the B-52 type aircraft, and low-level flight testing was resumed.

History of "Tommy's Tigator"

Built in 1957 by the Boeing Aircraft assembly plant in Wichita, Kansas, B-52D, serial number 56-0591, was one of several B-52s acquired by the U.S. Air Force for special purposes. Prior to the accident "Tommy's Tigator" had previously participated in "Operation Hardtac," during which nuclear tests were conducted at the Pacific Proving Ground between April 28 and August 18, 1958. The U.S. Air Force Air Materials Command and the Atomic Energy Commission detonated 35 nuclear devices at Bikini Atoll, Enewetak Atoll in the Marshall Islands, and Johnson Island in the Pacific Ocean. They included balloon, surface, underwater, and rocket-borne high-altitude tests.

Captain Tom Summer was the aircraft commander of Tommy's Tigator which was nicknamed by a joke about a very mean animal that was half tiger and half alligator, and the B-52D originally had a painting of a green tiger's head on its nose. It was this new B-52 Stratofortress that was chosen to be exposed to the nuclear blasts. Loaded with electronic monitoring equipment, 56-059 flew sorties above 20,000 feet through the radioactive atmosphere to collect radiation effects information during nine of the nuclear explosions.

The last mission that Summer's crew flew was conducted at low level during daylight in the mid-afternoon at an altitude of 500 feet above the surface. The day of this practice flight, the air was exceptionally turbulent and they bounced around the pattern at 425 knots indicated airspeed giving the airframe a terrible beating. They ran all of the instrumentation that measured everything and even though there was no heat or overpressure input from a bomb blast, there was plenty of airframe loading due to the turbulence. After landing they discovered large pieces of skin missing from the upper surface of both the left and right horizontal stabilizers. Each section had lost very sizable pieces two by three feet in dimension.

This caused a huge concern in determining what had happened. A fast review of the data from the loads-measuring instrumentation was conducted to determine if any of the structural members had been overloaded. The analysis of the data, conducted in consultation with the structural engineers in Seattle and the Aircraft Laboratory at Wright-Patterson AFB, indicated the airframe had not been overloaded.

The team of engineers was made up of many representatives from the Boeing Company, and they were all experienced analysts. Some of the representatives from the Aircraft Laboratory were engineers as well. The final analysis was that the damage experienced on the practice flight was only of a superficial nature and the airframe had not been subjected to forces beyond its structural limits. The recommendation was to "fly the profile as planned." As it turned out this was the wrong recommendation, but that was not discovered for nearly a year.

After the sheet metal on the horizontal stabilizers had been repaired, the mission went on as planned. On the day of the flight the air was smooth and the device gave a yield of about 10 megatons. Summer and his crew experienced from the explosion, the effects predicted and received no damage from turbulence.

After this flight was concluded, 56-059 was flown back to the Boeing factory in Seattle. The B-52D was then turned over to Boeing on a contract to conduct a lengthy series of flight investigations at low altitudes and high speeds. This particular aircraft was selected because of the elaborate loads-measuring instrumentation that had been installed for Hardtac.

A lengthy review of the data received on the late Tommy's Tigator from all missions flown, including that obtained during Hardtac, revealed that the method of predicting structural failure had been in error. It had been believed that the failure speed of the B-52 was much higher than 425 knots indicated airspeed, but the review indicated it was much closer to about 430, depending on turbulence. After all of this came out, the placard speed of the B-52 was lowered to about 350 knots indicated airspeed.

The loss of the Boeing crew involved in the crash of Tommy's Tigator hung heavily on the minds of everyone associated with it. The fact that this B-52D Stratofortress had previously been battered by nine nuclear and thermonuclear detonations made the loss even more poignant.

B-52D, 56-0591: Crash Site Today

In a very sparsely populated area of northcentral Oregon, our wreck hunting group was finally able to locate the crash site of "Tommy's Tigator." We had been researching this accident for several years and through the help of Dale Martin of Riley, Oregon; Ken Potter was able to meet with him and arrange for Dale to lead us to the wreck. Dale is an avid hunter in this area located thirty-five miles west of Burns, Oregon, and had known about the wreck for years. Our visit to the crash site located northwest of Riley required forty-five minutes driving time by four-wheel drive vehicles over rough terrain, and the crossing of a stream to reach a point close to the site. After starting up an incline for about an eighth of a mile, we started seeing debris and engine compressor blades. We then followed a line of debris to the main impact area and then into the canyon that the B-52 bomber had been flying in prior to the accident.

We found some debris about a quarter of a mile short of the main impact area indicating that some parts had separated from the bomber prior to the main bulk of the aircraft striking the ground. At the main impact area on top of a small plateau we noted there being a fairly heavy concentration of small heavily damaged pieces of debris originating from the nose and wings of the plane. This area extended for approximately three-hundred feet and was mostly void of any vegetation growth probably due to a heavy concentration of jet fuel spilled there. A second impact area approximately two-hundred feet beyond this point showed signs of severe burning where we found melted aluminum slag along with harness buckles, burned parachute material, and heavily burned steel hardware and radio parts. After disintegrating, the heavier wreckage had tumbled off the rocky edge of the plateau and travelled in several different directions. In one area to the southeast, we found pieces of engine pylons, wing parts, and where the cockpit appeared to have come to rest and burned. To the northeast, we had found where other parts had tumbled over a hill and created several other burn areas leaving mounds of aluminum slag and ash. In all, it appeared that the crash path extended for over a one mile distance across the high-desert sagebrush covered landscape. While looking down the canyon that the aircraft was flying in, it was hard for me to envision a large B-52 bomber flying at a high rate of speed below the canyon rim.

Boeing B-52D, 56-0591 "Tommy's Tigator" shining with Day-Glo trim along with a line-up of other Boeing aircraft including the very first KC-135A Stratotanker. This B-52 participated in Operation Hardtac and was destroyed in a test accident near Burns, Oregon shortly after this photo was taken. (Boeing Aircraft Company)

Dale Martin and Ken Potter inspect the remains of engine pods at the crash site of B-52D, 56-0591, which crashed 35 miles west of Burns, Oregon on June 23, 1959. (Photo by Dave McCurry)

Stainless steel engine pod from the crashed B-52, blued from heat coming off from one of its jet engines. (Photo by Dave McCurry)

Orange Day-Glo paint on this small piece of wreckage found where the nose of the large bomber had struck the ground. (Photo by Dave McCurry)

Small pieces of wreckage like the ones pictured littered the ground everywhere. (Photo by Dave McCurry)

Seat harness buckles found at the site. There were parts of burned parachute material found nearby also. (Photo by Dave McCurry)

Oil Pressure gauge that was located in the overhead eyebrow panel of the B-52D. (Photo by Dave McCurry)

Small piece of rudder pedal found by Ken Potter suggests a very severe nose impact. (Photo by Dave McCurry)

This appears to be a piece of the alternator pack circuit breaker panel which was located in the left forward wheel well. (Photo by Dave McCurry)

Wing rib with flap track from the B-52 was found near the end of the crash path. (Photo by Dave McCurry)

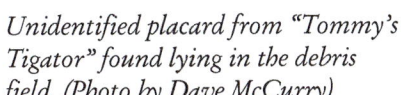

Unidentified placard from "Tommy's Tigator" found lying in the debris field. (Photo by Dave McCurry)

Vicki McCurry along with Ken Potter and Don Hinton inspect and photograph small pieces of wreckage at the crash site of B-52, 56-0591. Note the barren area to the right of the photo which was probably contaminated with jet fuel, never allowing much growth after the crash. (Photo by Dave McCurry)

Chapter 4

United Flight 173: Portland Oregon

By David L. McCurry

SYNOPSIS

AT about 1815 Pacific Standard Time on December 28, 1978, United Airlines Flight 173, crashed into a wooded populated area of suburban Portland, Oregon, during a landing approach to the Portland International Airport. The McDonnell-Douglas DC-8 airliner had delayed the landing while circling southeast of the airport at a low altitude for about one hour while the flight crew coped with a landing gear malfunction and prepared the passengers for a possible emergency landing. The plane crashed about 6 nautical miles southeast of the airport and was destroyed. There was no fire. Of the 181 passengers and 8 crewmembers aboard, 8 passengers, the flight engineer, and a flight attendant were killed, and 21 passengers plus 2 crewmembers were seriously injured.

The National Transportation Safety Board determined that the probable cause of this accident was the failure of the captain to monitor the aircraft's fuel status properly, to properly respond to the low fuel state, and the crewmember's advisories regarding the fuel state. This resulted in fuel exhaustion to all engines. This inattention resulted from preoccupation with a landing gear malfunction and preparations for a possible emergency landing.

Contributing to the accident was the failure of the other two flight crewmembers either to fully comprehend the criticality of the fuel state, or to successfully communicate their concern to the captain. It was incredibly amazing that anyone could have survived a nighttime crash landing like this!

HISTORY OF THE FLIGHT

On December 28, 1978, United Airlines, Inc., Flight 173, a McDonnell-Douglas DC-8-61, (N8082U), departed on a scheduled flight from John F. Kennedy International Airport, New York, to Portland International Airport, Portland, Oregon, with an en route stop at Denver, Colorado.

Flight 173, piloted by Captain Malburn A. McBroom along with First Officer Rodrick D. Beebe, and Flight Engineer Forrest E. Mendenhall, departed from Denver at about 1447 with 189 persons on board, including 6 infants, and 8 crewmembers. The flight was cleared to Portland on an instrument flight rules (IFR) flight plan. The planned time en route was two hours and twenty-six minutes. The planned arrival time at Portland was 1713.

An accident report filed by the National Transportation Safety Board listed several disorganizing effects related to a landing gear problem that finally led up to this accident, and it started with this account.

According to the automatic flight plan and monitoring system, the total amount of fuel required for the flight to Portland was 31,900 lbs. There was 46,700 lbs. of fuel on board the aircraft when it departed the gate at Denver. This fuel included the Federal Aviation Regulation requirement for fuel to destination plus 45 minutes reserve, and the company contingency fuel of about 20 minutes. During a post-accident interview, Captain McBroom stated that he was very close to his predicted fuel for the entire flight to Portland, or there would have been some discussion of it. The captain also explained that his flight from Denver to Portland was normal.

At 1705:47, Flight 173 called Portland Approach and advised that its altitude was 10,000 feet and its airspeed was being reduced. Portland Approach responded and told the flight to maintain its heading for a visual approach to runway 28. Flight 173 acknowledged the approach instructions and stated, "we have the field in sight."

At 1707:55, Portland Approach instructed the flight to descend and maintain 8,000 feet. Flight 173 acknowledged the instructions and advised that it was "leaving ten." At 1709:40, Flight 173 received and acknowledged a clearance to continue its descent to 6,000 feet.

During a post-accident interview, Captain McBroom stated that, when Flight 173 was descending through about 8,000 feet, First Officer Beebe, who was flying the aircraft, requested the wing flaps be extended to 15 degrees, then asked that the landing gear be lowered. Captain McBroom stated that he complied with both requests. However, he further-stated that as the landing gear extended, it was noticeably unusual and he felt that it seemed to go down more rapidly. As it was his recollection, it was a thump, thump in sound and feel. He didn't recall getting the red and transient gear door light. The thump was much out of the ordinary for this airplane. It was noticeably different and we got the nose gear green light but no other lights. Captain McBroom also said the first officer remarked that the aircraft "yawed to the right." Both flight attendant and passenger statements also indicated that there was a loud noise and a severe jolt when the landing gear was lowered.

At 1712:20, Portland Approach requested, "United one seven three 'heavy, contact the tower (Portland), one one eight point seven." The flight responded, "negative, we'll stay with you. We'll stay at five. We'll maintain about a hundred and seventy knots. We've got a gear problem. We'll let you know." This was the first indication to anyone on the ground that Flight 173 had a problem. At 1712:28, Portland Approach replied, "United one seventy-three heavy roger, maintain five thousand. Turn left heading two zero zero." The flight acknowledged the instructions.

At 1714:43, Portland Approach advised, "United one seventy-three heavy, turn left heading one zero zero, and I'll just orbit you out there till you get your problem." Flight 173 acknowledged the instructions.

For the next 23 minutes, while Portland Approach was vectoring the aircraft in a holding pattern south and east of the airport, the flight crew discussed and accomplished all of the emergency and precautionary actions available to them to assure themselves that all landing gears were locked in the full down position. The Flight Engineer, Forrest Mendenhall, checked the visual indicators on top of both wings, which extended above the wing surface when the landing gear is down and locked.

Captain McBroom also stated that during this same time period, the first flight attendant came forward and he discussed the situation with her. He told her that after they ran a few more checks, he would let her know what he intended to do.

About 1738, Flight 173 contacted the United Airlines Systems Line Maintenance Control Center in San Francisco, California, through Aeronautical Radio, Inc. According to recordings, at 1740:47 Captain McBroom explained to company dispatch and maintenance personnel the landing gear problem and what the flight crew had done to assure that the landing gear was fully extended. He reported about 7,000 lbs. of fuel on board and stated his intention to hold for another 15 or 20 minutes. He stated that he was going to have the flight attendants prepare the passengers for an emergency evacuation.

At 1744:03, United San Francisco asked, "okay, United one seventy three ... You estimate that you'll make a landing about five minutes past the hour. Is that okay?" Captain McBroom responded, "Ya, that's a good ball park. I'm not gonna hurry the girls. We got about a hundred sixty-five people on board, and we ...want to ...take our time and get everybody ready and then we'll go. It's clear as a bell and no problem."

The aircraft continued to circle under the direction of Portland Approach in a triangular pattern southeast of the airport at 5,000 ft. The pattern kept the aircraft within about 20 nautical miles of the airport.

From about 1744:30 until about 1745:23, the cockpit voice recorder (CVR) contained conversation between the captain and the first flight attendant concerning passenger preparation, crash landing procedures, and evacuation procedures. During his initial interview, Captain McBroom indicated that he neither designated a time limit to the flight attendant, nor asked her how long it would take to prepare the cabin. He stated that he assumed 10 or 15 minutes would be reasonable, and that some preparations could be made on the final approach to the airport.

At 1746:52, First Officer Beebe asked Flight Engineer Mendenhall, "How much fuel we got ... ?" The flight engineer responded, "Five thousand." The first officer acknowledged the response.

At 1748:38, Portland Approach advised Flight 173 that there was another aircraft in its vicinity. The first officer advised Portland Approach that he had the aircraft in sight.

At 1748:54, the first officer asked the captain, "What's the fuel show now ... ?" The captain replied, "Five." The first officer repeated, "Five." At 1749, after a partially unintelligible comment by the flight engineer concerning fuel pump lights, the captain stated, "That's about right, the feed pumps are starting to blink." According to data received from the manufacturer, the total usable fuel remaining when the inboard feed pump lights illuminate is 5,000 lbs. At this time, according to flight data recorder (FDR) and air traffic control data, the aircraft was about 13 nautical miles south of the airport on a west, southwesterly heading.

From just after 1749 until 1749:45, the flight crew engaged in further conversation about the status of the landing gear. This conversation was interrupted by a heading change from Portland Approach and was followed by a traffic advisory from Portland Approach.

About 1750:20, Captain McBroom asked Flight Engineer Mendenhall to "give us a current card on weight. Figure about another fifteen minutes." First Officer Beebe responded, "Fifteen minutes?" To which the captain replied, "Yeah, give us three or four thousand pounds on top of zero fuel weight." The flight engineer then said, "Not enough. Fifteen minutes is gonna really run us low on fuel here." At 1750:47, the flight engineer gave the following information for the landing data card. "Okay, take three thousand pounds, two hundred and four." At this time the aircraft was about 18 nautical miles south of the airport in a turn to the northeast.

At 1751:35, Captain McBroom instructed the flight engineer to contact the company representative at Portland and advise him of the situation and tell him that Flight 173 would land with about 4,000 lbs. of fuel. From 1752:17 until about 1753:30, the flight engineer talked to Portland and discussed the aircraft's fuel state, the number of persons on board the aircraft, and the emergency landing preparations at the airport.

At 1753:30, because of an inquiry from the company representative at Portland; Flight Engineer Mendenhall told Captain McBroom, "He wants to know if we'll be landing about five after." The captain replied, "Yes." The flight engineer relayed the captain's reply to the company representative. At this time the aircraft was about 17 nautical miles south of the airport heading northeast.

At 1755:04, Flight Engineer Mendenhall reported the "approach descent check is complete." At 1756:53, First Officer Beebe asked, "How much fuel you got now?" The flight engineer responded that 3,000 lbs. remained, 1,000 lbs. in each tank.

At 1757:21, Captain McBroom sent the flight engineer to the cabin to "kind of see how things are going..." From 1757:30 until 1800:50, the captain and the first officer engaged in a conversation which included discussions of giving the flight attendants ample time to prepare for the emergency cockpit procedures in the event of an evacuation after landing, whether the brakes would have antiskid protection after landing, and the procedures the captain would be using during the approach and landing.

At 1801:12, Portland Approach requested that the flight turn left to a heading of 195 degrees. First Officer Beebe acknowledged and complied with the request.

At 1801:34, Flight Engineer Mendenhall returned to the cockpit and reported that the cabin would be ready in "another two or three minutes." The aircraft was about 5 nautical miles southeast of the airport turning to a southwesterly heading. Until about 1802:10, the captain and the flight engineer discussed the passengers and their attitudes toward the emergency.

At 1802:22, Flight Engineer Mendenhall advised, "We got about three on the fuel and that's it." The aircraft was then about 5 nautical miles south of the airport on a southwest heading. Captain McBroom responded, "Okay, on touchdown, if the gear folds or something really jumps the track, get those boost pumps off so that...you might even get the valves open."

At 1802:44, Portland Approach asked Flight 173 for a status report and First Officer Beebe replied, "Yeah, we have an indication that our gear is abnormal. It'll be our intention, in about five minutes, to land on two-eight left. We would like the equipment standing by. Our indications are the gear is down and locked. We've got our people prepared for an evacuation in the event that it should become necessary."

At 1803:14, Portland Approach asked that Flight 173 advise them when the approach would begin. Captain McBroom responded, "They've about finished in the cabin. I'd guess about another three, four, five minutes." At this time the aircraft was about 8 nautical miles south of the airport on a southwesterly heading.

At 1803:23, Portland Approach asked Flight 173 for the number of persons on board and the amount of fuel remaining. Captain McBroom replied, "...about four thousand, well, make it three thousand pounds of fuel," and..., "you can add to that one-seventy-two plus six laps infants."

From 1803:38 until 1806:10, the flight crew engaged in a conversation which concerned checking the landing gear warning horn as further evidence that the landing gear was fully down and locked, and also whether automatic spoilers and antiskid would operate normally with the landing gear circuit breakers out.

At 1806:19, the first flight attendant entered the cockpit and Captain McBroom asked, "How you doing?" She responded, "Well, I think we're ready." At this time the aircraft was about 17 nautical miles south of the airport on a southwesterly heading. The conversation between the first flight attendant and the captain continued until about 1806:40 when Captain McBroom said, "Okay, we're going to go in now. We should be landing in about five minutes." Almost simultaneous with this comment, First Officer Beebe said, "I think you just lost number four ... ," followed immediately by advice to the flight engineer, "... better get some cross-feeds open there or something."

At 1806:46, First Officer Beebe told Captain McBroom, "We're going to lose an engine..." McBroom replied, "Why?" At 1806:49, the first officer again stated, "we're losing an engine." Again the captain asked, "Why?" The first officer responded, "Fuel." Between 1806:52 and 1807:06, the CVR revealed conflicting and confusing conversation between flight crew members as to the aircraft's fuel state. At 1807:06, First Officer Beebe said, "it's flamed out."

At 1807:12, Captain McBroom called Portland Approach and requested, "We would like clearance for an approach into two-eight left now." The aircraft was about 19 nautical miles south southwest of the airport and turning left. This was the first request for an approach clearance from Flight 173 since the landing gear problem began. Portland Approach immediately gave the flight vectors for a visual approach to runway 28L. The flight turned toward the vector heading of 010 degrees.

From 1807:27 until 1809:16, the following intra-cockpit conversation took place:

1807:27- Flight Engineer: "We're going to lose number three in a minute, too."
1807:31- Flight Engineer: "It's showing zero"
Captain: "You got a thousand pounds. You got to."
Flight Engineer: "Five thousand in there...but we lost it."
Captain: "Alright"
1807:38 - Flight Engineer: "Are you getting it back?"
1807:40 - First Officer: "No number four. You got that cross-feed open?"
1807:41- Flight Engineer: "No, I haven't got it open. "Which one?"
1807:42 - Captain: "Open 'em both—get some fuel in there. Got some fuel pressure?"
Flight Engineer: "Yes sir."
1807:48 - Captain: "Rotation. Now she's coming."
1807:52 - Captain: "Okay, watch one and two. We're showing down to zero or a thousand."
Flight Engineer: "Yeah."
Captain: "On number one?"
Flight Engineer: "Right."
1808:08 - First Officer: "Still not getting it."
1808:11 - Captain: "Well, open all four cross-feeds."
Flight Engineer: "All four?"
Captain: "Yeah."
1808:14 - First Officer: "Alright, now it's coming."
1808:19 - First Officer: "It's going to be ...on approach though."
Unknown Voice: "Yeah."
1808:42 - Captain: "You gotta keep em running..."
Flight Engineer: "Yes, sir."
1808:45 - First Officer: "Get this...on the ground."
Flight Engineer: "Yeah. It's showing not very much more fuel."
1809:16 - Flight Engineer: "We're down to one on the totalizer. Number two is empty."

At 1809:21, Captain McBroom advised Portland Approach, "United, seven three is going to turn toward the airport and come on in." After confirming Flight 173's intentions, Portland Approach cleared the flight for the visual approach to runway 28L.

At 1810:17, Captain McBroom requested that the flight engineer "reset that circuit breaker momentarily. See if we get gear lights." The flight engineer complied with the request.

At 1810:47, Captain McBroom requested the flight's distance from the airport. Portland approach responded, "I'd call it eighteen flying miles."

At 1812:42, Captain McBroom made another request for distance. Portland Approach responded, "Twelve flying miles." The flight was then cleared to contact Portland tower.

At 1813:21, Flight Engineer Mendenhall stated, "We've lost two engines guys."

At 1813:25, Mendenhall stated, "We just lost two engines, one and two."

At 1813:38, Captain McBroom said, "They're all going. We can't make Troutdale." First Officer Beebe said, "We can't make anything."

At 1813:46, Captain McBroom told First Officer Beebe, "Okay, declare a mayday."

At 1813:50, First Officer Beebe called Portland International Airport tower and declared, "Portland tower, United one seventy three heavy, Mayday! We're--the engines are flaming out. We're going down. We're not going to be able to make the airport." This was the last radio transmission from Flight 173.

About 1815, the aircraft crashed into a wooded section of a populated area of suburban Portland, about 6 nautical miles east southeast of the airport. There was no fire. The wreckage path was about 1,554 ft. long and about 130 ft. wide. The accident occurred during the hours of darkness at a latitude of 45.3121N, and longitude of 122.2959W. The elevation of the accident site was 285 ft.

WRECKAGE AND IMPACT INFORMATION

The aircraft first struck two trees about 100 ft. above the ground. These trees were about 1,554 ft. from the point where the wreckage came to rest.

About 541 ft. farther along the flight path on a heading of about 345 degrees, the aircraft struck two trees about 85 ft. above the ground. About 400 ft. farther, the right wing struck a tree about 45 feet above the ground. About 225 ft. beyond that point, the left outer wing struck a tree about 8 ft. above the ground. The aircraft then struck and destroyed an unoccupied house which was located about 1,230 ft. from the first tree. Pieces of the aircraft's left wing structure were located just beyond the house.

The two main landing gears and the nose section of the aircraft first struck a 5 foot embankment next to E. Burnside street about 1,275 ft. from the first tree. The aircraft continued across the street and came to rest on a heading of 330 degrees between some trees and on top of another unoccupied house. The tail of the aircraft came to rest about 1,350 ft. from the first tree. Just after crossing the street, the vertical stabilizer struck a series of high tension cables, which ran parallel to the street.

The fuselage, from about the fifth row of passenger seats forward, sustained severe extensive impact damage in a generally rearward direction. The cockpit upper structure, which included the cockpit forward windows, had separated and was found to the right of the fuselage just forward of the inboard end of the right wing. The cockpit floor structure, which included portions of the crew seats, sections of the instrument panel, and the nose tunnel structure with the nose gear assembly partially attached, had separated and rotated to the right and aft. This structure was in a partially inverted position. All portions of the fuselage structure were accounted for and all of the structural damage was caused by impact with the ground and the numerous large trees in the immediate area.

The lower left side of the fuselage, between the fourth and sixth rows of passenger seats and below window level, had been torn away. The remainder of the underside of the fuselage sustained heavy damage from contact with several large trees and tree stumps. The passenger cabin interior, from row 6 to the aft bulkhead, was relatively intact. At several points along the fuselage, windows were smashed and the fuselage had been dented by large trees and separated portions of the main landing gear.

The empennage showed moderate impact damage. The vertical stabilizer leading edge had been damaged by high tension cables at three points just forward of the upper three rudder-to-stabilizer hinge points.

The left wing had separated from the fuselage about 3 ft. outboard from the fuselage attachment point. The No. 2 engine had separated from its pylon and was located adjacent to the wing trailing edge. The No. 1 engine remained attached to a section of the left wing structure. A 7 foot long section of the left wingtip had been sheared off and was found near the first house.

The right wing separated about 5 ft. from the fuselage. A two foot opening was evident between the fuselage and wing leading edge structure. The wing leading edge, from a point about 5 ft. outboard from the leading edge inboard end, was cut and torn aft to the front spar assembly. A large section of the right wing leading edge structure had separated during the impact sequence and was also found near the first house.

A section of right wing with the No. 3 engine and pylon attached was located just forward of the right horizontal stabilizer. The outboard wing section, which included the No. 4 engine, was to the right of the fuselage.

All four engines were inspected and found to be capable of operation. None showed signs of rotation at impact.

Both main landing gears were fully extended but were torn from their mounting structures. They were located near the main wreckage. Inspection of the right main landing gear retraction mechanism showed corrosion in the threads of an attachment eyebolt. The eyebolt was pulled out of the actuator cylinder piston. The nose landing gear was fully extended and remained attached to the nose tunnel structure.

Survival Aspects

The accident was partially survivable. The 10 occupants killed in the crash which included Flight Engineer Forrest Mendenhall, were located between the flight engineer's station in the cockpit and row 5 in the passenger cabin. All of the passengers who were killed had been located on the right side of the cabin. That section of the aircraft was destroyed during the accident sequence.

The most seriously injured passengers were seated in the right forward portion of the cabin near an area of the fuselage which appeared to have been penetrated by a large tree. These persons were seated near those passengers who were injured fatally. Some seriously injured passengers were seated in the rear cabin near the trailing edge of the wings. The fuselage in this area had been penetrated and the floor and seats had been disrupted.

Several passengers later on reflected that communication in the rear of the plane was poor but they did hear the flight crew announcing for passengers to brace themselves for the landing. In preparation for a crash landing, several strong men had been staged at the emergency exits and babies were placed on the floor next to cabin partitions so they wouldn't be thrown forward when the plane crashed. The powerless glide toward a small dark unlighted patch in the neighborhood near 157th and E. Burnside Street was quiet and seemed peaceful to some of the passengers on board. There were people up ahead putting on coats and getting out blankets, so everyone in the rear of the plane copied them and did the same. There was no real panic in the tail section and passengers sitting there remembered looking out of the windows and seeing street lights and houses very near them. With the engines not producing power, it was very quiet and some passengers were heard to holler out to others "get into the crash position." Suddenly the sound of the jetliner's wings clipping trees could be heard followed by a jolt and the sounds of a vacant rental house being smashed apart on the south side of Burnside Street. You could hear the sounds of the wing ripping into the roof and hear several large booms as the plane lurched around from hitting the house and then after hitting several large fir trees. Along with that, the sounds of aluminum tearing could be heard as the plane's wing was being sheared off by large fir trees. Realizing what was happening, passengers started burying their heads in their coats. The plane's nose had dug into a five foot embankment and then collided with a large fir tree destroying the first five rows of the nose section. It was very quiet and still when the aircraft came to a stop. Then passengers found an exit at the rear of the plane and started jumping to the ground. It was the end of the holiday and many passengers were coming home from Christmas travels.

After running outside to see what had happened, residents living a few doors away from the crash site of United Flight 173 stated that everything went very black and there were house fragments and insulation lying everywhere. There had been no major crashing sounds, just a whoosh and the sound of snapping trees and falling debris. The nearby residents were shocked when they walked out and saw the huge "United" insignia on the vertical stabilizer sticking up in the darkness surrounded by broken trees. As some of the local residents rushed over to help people from the plane, they heard some of the passengers asking where the terminal was, thinking that they were at the airport. After helping some of the passengers off the plane, distant sirens could be heard coming from all directions. Medical personnel arriving on the scene then quickly took over the rescue operations. As the local residents stood and watched the remaining passengers being helped off the plane, they related to each other how fortunate they were considering that miraculously no one on the ground had been injured.

After being captured in Denver, Colorado, escaped prisoner Kim Edward Campbell was being escorted back to the Oregon State Penitentiary in Salem, Oregon on board Flight 173. He had walked away from the Oregon Corrections Division's forestry work camp at Tillamook on January 21, 1978 with 14 months remaining on a four year sentence for robbery. He was real scared but stayed around after the crash helping passengers.

Capt. Roger Seed who was escorting Campbell back to Oregon said that after finding an opening, he jumped about eight feet to the ground while Campbell handed passengers down to him. When the passengers stopped coming out, Campbell helped Capt. Seed back into the plane and did a quick check to see if anyone else was left. Seed stated that Campbell helped out more than a lot of other people would. After all of the passengers had been pulled to safety, and throughout all of the confusion and darkness, Campbell took advantage of the crash to gain his freedom again.

Governor Tom McCall stated that because of his help with stabilizing and transporting victims, and due to the non-violent nature of his crimes as well as his obvious concern for others, Kim Campbell was welcome to remain in Oregon as long as he wished, and was given a Governor's Pardon.

Some passengers sustained serious injuries during the evacuation. Two passengers sustained fractures and others sustained lacerations and abrasions when they either fell from exits or as they climbed through debris outside of the aircraft in order to reach the ground. As a result of the accident, 22 persons were admitted to hospitals with serious injuries ranging from multiple fractures of extremities and fractures of cervical vertebrae, to observations for possible injuries.

The plane crashed in the jurisdiction of Multnomah County Rural Fire Protection District No. 10. Three fire departments sent personnel and equipment to the scene. The Port of Portland (Airport) Fire Department, Multnomah RFPD No. 10, and the City of Portland Fire Bureau. A total of 39 fire units and 108 on-duty fire personnel responded to the scene. Numerous off-duty fire personnel from all fire departments also responded to the scene. Because there was no fire, the basic fire service functions were search and rescue, extrication, triage, emergency medical care, precautionary foaming of some aircraft parts and surrounding area, laying standby firefighting water supply lines, transporting or assisting ambulatory victims to a nearby church, setting up area lighting, providing some interagency radio communications, and setting up the on-scene command post.

Although there were many occupied houses and apartment complexes in the immediate vicinity of the accident, there were no ground casualties and no post-crash fire. Injured persons were transported to nearby hospitals by helicopter and ambulance.

RESOLVING A PROBLEM

The NTSB's report stated that the first problem which faced the captain of Flight 173 was the unsafe landing gear indication during the initial approach to Portland International Airport. This unsafe indication followed a loud thump, an abnormal vibration, and an abnormal aircraft yaw as the landing gear was lowered. The Safety Board's investigation revealed that the landing gear problem was caused by severe corrosion in the mating threads where the right main landing gear retract cylinder assembly actuator piston rod was connected to the rod end. The corrosion allowed the two parts to pull apart and the right main landing gear to fall free when the flight crew lowered the landing gear. This rapid fall disabled the micro switch for the right main landing gear which completes an electrical circuit to the gear position indicators in the cockpit. The difference between the time it took for the right main landing gear to free fall and the time it took for the left main landing gear to extend normally, probably created a difference in aerodynamic drag for a short time. This difference in drag produced a transient yaw as the landing gear dropped.

Although the landing gear malfunction precipitated a series of events which culminated in the accident, the established company procedures for dealing with landing gear system failure(s) on the DC-8-61 are adequate to permit the safest possible operation and landing of the aircraft. Training procedures, including ground school, flight training, and proficiency and recurrent training, direct the flight crew to the Irregular Procedures section of the DC-8 Flight Manual, which must be in the possession of crewmembers while in flight. The Irregular Procedures section instructed the crew to determine the position of both the main and nose landing gear visual indicators. "If the visual indicators indicate the gear is down, then a landing can be made at the captain's discretion." The flight engineer's check of the visual indicators for both main landing gear showed that they were down and locked. A visual check of the nose landing gear could not be made because the light which would have illuminated the down-and-locked visual indicator was not operating. However, unlike the main landing gear cockpit indicators, the cockpit indicator for the nose gear gave the proper "green gear down" indication.

Admittedly, the abnormal gear extension was cause for concern and a flight crew should assess the situation before communicating with the dispatch or maintenance personnel. However, aside from the crew's discussing the problem and adhering to the DC-8 Flight Manual, the only remaining step was to contact company dispatch and line maintenance. From the time the captain informed Portland Approach of the gear problem until contact with company dispatch and line maintenance, about 28 minutes had elapsed. The irregular gear check procedures contained in their manual were brief, the weather was good, the area was void of heavy traffic, and there were no additional problems experienced by the flight that would have delayed the captain's communicating with the company. The company maintenance staff verified that everything possible had been done to assure the integrity of the landing gear. Therefore, upon termination of communications with company dispatch and maintenance personnel, which was about thirty minutes before the crash, the captain would have made a landing attempt. The Safety Board believes that flight 173 could have landed safely within 30 to 40 minutes after the landing gear malfunction.

The Safety Board believed that any time a flight had deviated from a flight plan, the flight crew should evaluate the potential effect of such deviation on the aircraft fuel status. This flight crew knew that the evaluation of the landing gear problem and preparation for an emergency landing would require extended holding before landing.

The flight crew should have been aware that there was 46,700 lbs. of fuel aboard the aircraft when it left Denver at 1433 and that there was about 45,650 lbs. at takeoff at 1447. Regardless of whether they were aware of the actual fuel quantities, they certainly should have been aware that the initial fuel load was predicated on fuel consumption for the planned 2 hour 26 minute en route flight, plus a reserve which includes sufficient fuel for 45 minutes at normal cruise and a contingency margin of about 20 minutes additional flight.

Therefore, the crew should have known and should have been concerned that fuel could become critical after holding. Proper crew management includes constant awareness of fuel remaining as it relates to time. In fact, the Safety Board believed that proper planning would provide for enough fuel on landing for a go-around should it become necessary. Such planning should also consider possible fuel-quantity indication inaccuracies. This would necessitate establishing a deadline time for initiating the approach and constant monitoring of time, as well as the aircraft's position relative to the active runway. Such procedures should be routine for all flight crews. However, based on available evidence, this flight crew did not adhere to such procedures. On the contrary, the cockpit conversation indicated insufficient attention and lack of awareness on the part of the captain about the aircraft's fuel state after entering and even after a prolonged period of holding.

The other two flight crewmembers, although they made several comments regarding the aircraft's fuel state, did not express direct concern regarding the amount of time remaining to total fuel exhaustion. While there is evidence to indicate that the crew was aware of the amount of fuel remaining at various times, there is no evidence that the onboard quantity was monitored in relation to time remaining during the final thirty minutes of flight. The Safety Board believed that had the flight crew been aware of the fuel state, comments concerning time to fuel exhaustion would have been voiced. However, there was none until after the aircraft was already in a position from which recovery was not possible.

In analyzing the flight crew's actions, the Safety Board considered that the crew could have been misled by inaccuracies within the fuel-quantity measuring system. However, those intra-cockpit comments and radio transmissions in which fuel quantity was mentioned indicate that the fuel-quantity indicating system was accurate.

Had the flight crew related any of these fuel quantities to fuel flow, they should have been aware that fuel exhaustion would occur at or about 1815. Other evidence that the captain had failed to assess the effect of continued holding on fuel state was provided by his stated intentions to land about 1805 with 4,000 lbs. of fuel on board. Just minutes earlier, at 1748:56, he was made aware that only 5,000 lbs. remained. During the 16 minutes between the observation of 5,000 lbs. and 1805, the aircraft would consume at least 3,000 lbs. of fuel. Further evidence of the flight crew's lack of concern or awareness was provided when just after his observations of 4,000 lbs. remaining about 17 minutes before the crash, the flight engineer left the cockpit at the captain's request to check on the cabin emergency evacuation preparations. Upon his return, about 4 minutes later, he gave the captain an estimate of another two or three minutes for the completion of the cabin preparation. At this time, the aircraft was in the general vicinity of the airport. In the initial interview with the captain, he stated that he felt the cabin preparation could be completed in from ten to fifteen minutes and that the "tail end of it" could be accomplished on the final approach to the airport. Certainly there was nothing more to do in the cockpit. All of the landing gear check procedures, as prescribed in the approved flight manual and recommended by company line maintenance, had been completed and dispatch had been notified and had alerted Portland company personnel of the problems.

Under these circumstances, there appeared to have been no valid reason not to discontinue their heading inbound toward the airport in order to make their previously estimated landing time. However, about 1801:12, the first officer accepted and the captain did not question a vector heading which would take them away from the airport and delay their landing time appreciably. Moreover, after the turn was completed, none of the flight crew suggested turning toward the airport. Thus, it was at this time that the crew's continuing preoccupation with the landing gear problem and landing preparations became crucial and an accident became inevitable.

The Safety Board also considered the possibility that the captain was aware of the fuel quantity on board, but failed to relate the fuel state to time and distance from the airport and intentionally extended the flight to reduce the fuel load in order to reduce the potential of fire should the landing gear fail upon landing. The Safety Board could find no evidence, however, to support such a theory and believes that had he so intended, the captain would have advised the first officer and the flight engineer. Therefore, the Safety Board can only conclude that the flight crew failed to relate the fuel remaining and the rate of fuel flow to the time and distance from the airport, because their attention was directed almost entirely toward diagnosing the landing gear problem. Although on two occasions the captain confirmed with the company that he intended to land about 1805 and that he would be landing with about 4,000 lbs. of fuel, this estimated time of arrival and landing fuel load were not adhered to, nor was the expected approach time given to Portland Approach. This failure to adhere to the estimated time of arrival and landing fuel loads strengthens the Board's belief that the landing gear problem had a seemingly disorganizing effect on the flight crew's performance. Evidence indicates that their scan of the instruments probably narrowed as their thinking fixed on the gear. After the number 4 engine had flamed out and with the fuel totalizer indicating 1,000 lbs., the captain was still involved in resetting circuit breakers to recheck landing gear light indications.

It was not until after it became apparent to the crew that total engine flame out was imminent that the captain was concerned, and in fact, may have been confused as to the amount of fuel which actually remained. About six minutes before all engines stopped, the captain stated that there was 1,000 lbs. of fuel in the number 1 main tank, and the flight engineer agreed with him. At this same time, the captain began to describe the gage indication as changing from 1,000 lbs. to zero lbs. Since the number 1 main tank gage does not change its indication from 1,000 lbs. to zero lbs. directly, but decreases in increments of 100 lbs., the captain must have read the gage indication incorrectly. Actually, the action he described was that of a gage changing from 100 lbs. to zero lbs.

The company had recently changed the fuel quantity gauges on this aircraft from a direct reading digital-type to a three-figure indicator that had to be multiplied by a factor of 100 to get the actual individual tank values. In addition, the new totalizer gage, of the same three-figure presentation as the individual tank gages, had to be multiplied by a factor of 1,000 to get the actual total fuel. During the stressed situation, the captain and the flight engineer may have mixed up these multipliers and used 1,000 when reading the individual tank gauges instead of 100. However, there was no evidence from previous comments that such a mistake was made. By the time such confusion was indicated; the accident was inevitable.

The Safety Board believed that this accident exemplified a recurring problem; a breakdown in cockpit management and teamwork during a situation involving malfunctions of aircraft systems in flight. To combat this problem, responsibilities must be divided among members of the flight crew while a malfunction was being resolved. In this case, apparently no one was specifically delegated the responsibility of monitoring fuel state.

Although the captain is in command and responsible for the performance of his crew, the actions or inactions of the other two flight crewmembers must be analyzed.

Admittedly, the stature of a captain and his management style may exert subtle pressure on his crew to conform to his way of thinking. It may hinder interaction and adequate monitoring and force another crewmember to yield his right to express an opinion.

The first officer's main responsibility is to monitor the captain. In particular, he provides feedback for the captain. If the captain infers from the first officer's actions or inactions that his judgment is correct, the captain could receive reinforcement for an error or poor judgment. Although the first officer did, in fact, make several subtle comments questioning or discussing the aircraft's fuel state, it was not until after the number 4 engine flamed out that he expressed a direct view, "Get this ... on the ground." Before that time, the comments were not given in a positive or direct tone. If the first officer recognized the criticality of the situation, he failed to convey these thoughts to the captain in a timely manner.

The flight engineer's responsibility, aside from management of the aircraft systems, is to monitor the captain's and first officer's actions as they pertain to the performance of the aircraft, that is, takeoff, landing, holding speeds, and range of the aircraft considering time and fuel flow. Although he informed the captain at 1750:30 that an additional "fifteen minutes is really gonna run us low on fuel here," there was no indication that he took affirmative action to insure that the captain was fully aware of the time to fuel exhaustion. Neither is there an indication that, upon returning to the cockpit at 1801:39, he relayed any concern about the aircraft's fuel state to the captain. Although he commented that 3,000 lbs. of fuel remained, he failed to indicate time remaining or his views regarding the need to expedite the landing.

The first officer's and the flight engineer's inputs on the flight deck are important because they provide redundancy. The Safety Board believed that, in training of all airline cockpit and cabin crewmembers, assertiveness training should be a part of the standard curricula, including the need for individual initiative and effective expression of concern.

In order to determine whether the captain had received all available assistance during the emergency, the Safety Board evaluated the actions of the company dispatcher and his role relative to the accident sequence. According to the tape of the conversation between the captain, the company dispatcher, and company line maintenance personnel, the captain had advised the dispatcher that he had 7,000 lbs. of fuel aboard and that he intended to land in 15 or 20 minutes. The dispatcher then checked with the captain to ascertain a specific time for the landing and the captain agreed that 1805 was "a good ballpark." The dispatcher, according to his interview after the accident, then relayed this landing time and the aircraft's status to the company personnel in Portland. He also stated that his assessment of the situation was that of the fuel remaining upon landing would be low but the landing could be made successfully at 1805. The Safety Board believed that, with the information given to him by the captain, the dispatcher acted properly and in accordance with company procedures.

FINDINGS

1. The flight crew was properly certificated and qualified for the flight.
2. The aircraft was certificated, maintained, and dispatched in accordance with Federal Aviation Regulations and approved company procedures.
3. Except for the failure of the piston rod on the right main landing gear retract cylinder assembly, with the resulting damage to the landing gear position indicating system switch, there was no evidence of a failure or malfunction of the aircraft's structure, power plants, flight controls, or systems.
4. The aircraft departed Denver with the required fuel aboard of 2 hours 26 minutes for the en route flight and with the required FAR and company contingency fuel aboard of about 1 hour.
5. The aircraft began holding about 1712 at 5,000 ft. With its gear down; this was about 2 hours 24 minutes after it departed Denver.
6. The landing delay covered a period of about 1 hour 2 minutes.
7. All of the aircraft's engines flamed out because of

fuel exhaustion at about 1815, 1 hour 3 minutes after it entered into the hold, and 3 hours 27 minutes after it had departed Denver.
8. Fuel exhaustion was predictable. The crew failed to equate the fuel remaining with time and distance from the airport.
9. No pertinent malfunctions were found during examinations of the fuel quantity measuring system.
10. A new digital fuel-quantity indicating system was installed on this aircraft on May 12, 1978. This was in accordance with a DC-8 UAL fleet wide retrofit program.
11. Evidence indicates that the fuel quantity indicating-system accurately indicated fuel quantity to the crew.
12. The fuel gages are readily visible to the captain and the second officer.
13. The captain failed to make decisive timely decisions.
14. The captain failed to relate time, distance from the airport, and the aircraft's fuel state as his attention was directed completely toward the diagnosis of the gear problem and preparation of the passengers for an emergency landing. The gear problem had a disorganizing effect on the captain's performance.
15. Neither the First Officer nor the Flight Engineer conveyed any concern about fuel exhaustion to the captain until the accident was inevitable.

PROBABLE CAUSE

The National Transportation Safety Board determined that the probable cause of the accident was the failure of the captain to monitor properly the aircraft's fuel state and to properly respond to the low fuel state and the crew-member's advisories regarding fuel state. This resulted in fuel exhaustion to all engines. His inattention resulted from preoccupation with a landing gear malfunction and preparations for a possible landing emergency.

Contributing to the accident was the failure of the other two flight crewmembers either to fully comprehend the criticality of the fuel state or to successfully communicate their concern to the captain.

The last NTSB recommendation following the incident, addressing flight-deck resource management problems, was the genesis for major changes in the way airline crewmembers were trained. This new type of training addressed behavioral management challenges such as poor crew coordination, loss of situational awareness, and judgment errors frequently observed in aviation accidents. It is credited with launching the Crew Resource Management (CRM) revolution in airline training.

Within weeks of the NTSB recommendation, NASA held a conference to bring government and industry experts together to examine the potential merits of this training. United Airlines instituted the industry's first Crew Resource Management/Cockpit Resource Management program for pilots in 1981. The CRM program proved to be so successful that it is now used throughout the world. The training was originally called Cockpit Resource Management, then Flightdeck Resource Management, but ultimately, Crew Resource Management became the universally accepted term. Since the United 173 crash resulted in the CRM training revolution, the accident has been called one of the most important in history.

UNITED FLIGHT 173: CRASH SITE TODAY

The crash site of United Flight 173 located at 15839 East Burnside Street, Portland, Oregon, is now home to the Windsor Court Apartment complex. Several rows of these apartments occupy the final resting place of the United Airlines DC-8-61, N8082U. Across the street on the south side of Burnside Street, the lot that the DC-8 crashed onto destroying an unoccupied home is still undeveloped looking much the same as it did after the accident minus the debris from the destroyed home. Residents still living near this area still have the memory of that tragic night of December 28, 1978 etched into their memories forever. Speaking to some of the locals you get a sense of them reliving the accident as if it only happened a week ago. Standing in the open lot looking north into the apartment complex, you get an eerie feeling imagining a huge four-engine jetliner of this size landing in this residential area at night, inflicting only ten fatalities onboard the aircraft, and none on the ground. It is incredible that 179 passengers and crew survived this accident and you get a sense that if the nose of this DC-8 had missed hitting the huge fir trees straight on, maybe everyone on board would have survived.

United Airlines Douglas DC-8-61, N8070U, as it taxies out for departure from the San Francisco International Airport. This airliner was an identical sister ship to United Flight 173's DC-8-61, N8082U, which crashed while maneuvering to land at the Portland International Airport, Portland, Oregon on December 28, 1978. (Photo by Richard Silagi)

The crash area of United Flight 173 as it was cordoned off just prior to the NTSB investigation. (Chris Baird collection)

Multnomah County Sherriff's Department helps secure the area while the investigation into the crash of United Flight 173 was under way. (Chris Baird collection)

The pile of rubble is part of the first class section from N8082U that flipped under the airliner when it crossed Burnside Avenue. This picture was taken after they lifted the plane and pulled the rubble out from under the front of the fuselage. (Photo by Jeff Schroeder)

Another shot of the same rubble pile from another angle. In this view you can see a seat or two. The cockpit was also somewhere in this rubble pile. (Photo by Jeff Schroeder)

More of the rubble pulled from under the DC-8-61. You can see in this photo the crane that was used to lift the plane. (Photo by Jeff Schroeder)

Shot of what was left of the nose of N8082U. The seats that are in the foreground, sit where they landed after being thrown from the plane. (Photo by Jeff Schroeder)

In this photo taken further back, you can see seats in the center, in front of the nose landing gear, and more seats just to the right of the "Keep Out" sign. There were passengers seated in those seats when they landed there, but it is not known whether they survived or not. (Photo by Jeff Schroeder)

Photo is of a crane operator removing the right main landing gear from the DC-8's wreckage. You can see several parts of the right wing; the first crushed up against the tree on the left side of the photo, then on the right side is the remainder of the wing with the right engine still attached. (Photo by Jeff Schroeder)

The right wing was sheared off just outside of the wing root after striking and shearing off several large trees. (Photo by Jeff Schroeder)

Shot of the main outboard portion of the right wing including the engine and pylon which may have spun a couple of times before coming to rest there? It is believed that the person in the photo was an NTSB investigator. (Photo by Jeff Schroeder)

Today the Windsor Court Apartments located at 15839 E. Burnside in Portland, Oregon occupy the crash site of Flight 173; N8082U, United Airlines DC-8-61. (Photo by Dave McCurry)

The white house with blue trim on the left side of the photo was next door to the crash site of Flight 173 and was shown on many newscasts as well as in newspaper photos. The Windsor Court Apartments are on the right center of the photo. (Photo by Dave McCurry)

An original aerial photo of the crash site of United Flight 173 in Portland, Oregon, taken by the Sheriff's office, shows many bystanders on the left of the photo observing the wreck of the DC-8-61 airliner. Note the white house on the corner to the left of the tail of the DC-8 which is still there today. (Multnomah County Archives)

The crash path of United Flight 173 today looking north into the Windsor Court Apartments. This empty lot looks much the same today as it did after the accident minus the debris left over from an unoccupied home destroyed by the DC-8 airliner. (Photo by Dave McCurry)

Chapter 5

Missing F4F Wildcats Found

By David L. McCurry

ON January 23, 1944, the United States Navy Squadron VC-80 which was commissioned at Sand Point Naval Air Station, Seattle, Washington, in December of 1943, was in the process of ferrying its planes from Sand Point to NAS North Bend, Oregon. This squadron consisted of 12 Grumman TBM Avenger torpedo planes and 16 Grumman F4F Wildcat fighter planes. The weather for this ferry flight was overcast and not the best of flying conditions but was forecast to be better along the route. The flight was dispatched to fly to Portland, Oregon, refuel, and then continue on to North Bend.

Later that day it was learned that not all of the planes had made it to Portland. Some had landed at other airfields, one had landed wheels-up in a farm field, and two F4F Wildcats were missing.

After a Visual Flight Rules (VFR) departure, the group of planes proceeded south headed toward Portland where they were to refuel before continuing on to their destination being North Bend. Just south of Toledo, Washington, the group of planes entered a large squall at which time they dropped below the level of the tops of mountains in the area. Engulfed in sleet and clouds, the planes bounced around in turbulence and were separated into small groups while attempting to navigate on their own toward their destination.

Ensign Ray Crandall who was flying one of the TBMs had better radio navigation equipment aboard his plane and found himself leading five or six planes. Some of the planes had a variety of mechanical problems with one of them being flown by the squadron commander, Lieutenant Stubbs, who was flying without a radio transmitter. Using an RDF (radio direction finder); Ensign Crandell navigated on this radio beacon toward Portland.

Lt. Stubbs spotted a landing field through a hole in the clouds and motioned the group to land at what turned out to be the airport in Toledo, Washington. After landing in Toledo, the pilots and crew were treated well by people of the town and were fed and put up for the night. During their stay, anxious phone calls were made by the crews trying to locate the rest of the squadron. The following day, January 24th, Lt. Stubb's group of planes was able to continue to Portland and then on to North Bend.

Two F4F-4 Wildcats (Bureau Numbers 03426 and 05077) flown by Lieutenant John R. Crowe and Ensign Joseph W. Schieche remained grouped together with other squadron planes and flew west towards the coast in an effort to try to navigate around the storm. The weather was better along the coast but the ground was blanketed in fog. At this point, the planes turned inland again climbing to an altitude high enough to clear the mountains and headed in the general direction of the Columbia River. When storm clouds closed in around them, the squadron suddenly broke up, and the last anyone had seen of Lt. Crowe and Ensign Schieche; they were headed over the Willapa Hills. Some of the other planes in this group were able to land in Astoria, Oregon, while the rest made it to Portland.

A few days after leaving Seattle, all of the squadron's planes were accounted for except those of Lt. Crowe and Ensign Schieche. Several theories abounded, but nothing was found of the two Wildcat fighter planes until five years later. Meanwhile, the VC-80 squadron was sent to San Diego, California, and then shipped off to Hawaii where they went aboard the USS Manila Bay. After fighting battles in the Philippines, the squadron was shipped back to San Diego in February of 1945 never knowing what had happened to Lt. Crowe and Ensign Schieche.

F4F Wildcat: Crash Sites Today

Wreckage of one of the two missing F4F Wildcat planes was found 18 miles southwest of Chehalis, Washington, and was first spotted on May 3, 1949 by Robert E. Manning, a Weyerhaeuser Timber Company surveyor. The plane was pinned under a large tree that was uprooted by the crash, or had fallen shortly afterward. On the afternoon of May 4th, Joe Chystil, Lewis County coroner, established that the pilot was Ensign Joseph W. Schieche by finding his identification in his badly decomposed wallet, and also his dog tags. Other personal effects including his watch were also found at the site. Ensign Schieche's remains were then recovered and sent to Spokane, Washington, where his parents were residing. The completely demolished remains of the plane were found by Manning's crew in dense timber and in a deep canyon as they were running a line 500 feet off a logging road.

One week later on May 9th, the second missing F4F Wildcat plane was found less than one-half mile away from the first plane at a higher elevation by someone on Robert Manning's survey crew. The plane had exploded and burned on impact leaving only very little scattered pieces at the crash site. The body of Lt. Crowe was never found, but a wrist watch and dog tags belonging to him were found.

The planes had crashed into a west facing hillside and this would have been the last ridge the planes would have had to clear before heading into the Chehalis Valley.

The crash sites of both planes were logged during the 1950s and 1960s and much of the remaining parts of the two planes were salvaged by loggers working in the area without much thought of removing pieces from the sites. After logging operations were completed, the sites were replanted and eventually forgotten.

Ensign Schieche's plane had served at Pearl Harbor, Hawaii, in 1942, and Lt. Crowe's plane had stayed on the mainland. Both planes were old with prior accident histories, and after being retired, were being used as training planes.

Today there are two nice granite memorial markers placed on Weyerhaeuser property marking the crash sites of Ensign Joseph W. Schieche and Lt. John R. Crowe's planes. There is not a lot of wreckage left from either of the planes at the two sites, but there is enough left to tell that they were both Navy F4F Wildcat fighter planes.

Grumman F4F Wildcat (at left) on display at the Tillamook Air Museum in Tillamook, Oregon. The U.S. Navy Wildcat did not meet the standards of the Japanese Zero, but it was a huge contribution to the war effort. Powered by a 1,200 horsepower Wright R-1830-36 radial piston engine, it had a 317 mph maximum speed, and was armed with six wing-mounted .50 caliber Browning machine-guns. (Photo by Dave McCurry)

Two Grumman F4F Wildcat planes piloted by Ensign Joseph W. Schieche and Lieutenant John R. Crowe disappeared on a ferry flight after departing Sandpoint NAS, Seattle, Washington on January 23, 1944, and were found five years later in May of 1949, southwest of Chehalis, Washington. Pictured are some of the remains of Lt. Crowe's plane. (Shawna Whelan Photography)

Very little remains today at the crash site of Lieutenant John R. Crowe's Grumman F4F Wildcat fighter plane. Loggers had cleaned up most of the wreckage in the 1950s. (Shawna Whelan Photography)

Looking uphill at some of the larger parts of John R. Crowe's Grumman F4F Wildcat fighter plane. The F4F Wildcat flown by Ensign Joseph W. Schieche was found one-half mile from this location in the mountains southwest of Chehalis, Washington. (Shawna Whelan Photography)

Granite memorial marker placed by Jim Ward at the F4F Wildcat crash site of Lieutenant John R. Crowe. (Shawna Whelan Photography)

Jim Ward beside the cross and granite marker placed at the crash site of Lt. John R. Crowe's Grumman F4F Wildcat fighter plane. (Photo by Frank Jongenburger)

More mangled parts of Lt. Crowe's plane scattered in the thick brush. (Photo by Jim Ward)

Granite marker before it was placed at the crash site of Ensign Joseph W. Schieche's F4F Wildcat fighter plane. (Photo by Jim Ward)

Michael Ward, Matt Comisky, and Jim Ward, (left to right) work together pulling a sled with the granite marker on top, downhill to be placed at the crash site of Ensign Schieche's F4F Wildcat plane. (Photo by Patty Ward)

The completed memorial for Ensign Schieche with cross and granite marker placed at the crash site. (Photo by Jim Ward)

Mangled parts from Ensign Schieche's F4F Wildcat plane with a rudder pedal in view on the right center of the photo. (Photo by Jim Ward)

Piece of wreckage from the Wildcat's fuselage still showing part of the navy insignia. (Photo by Jim Ward)

The Wildcat's 1,200 horsepower Wright R-1830 engine was missing, but one of its cylinders was still located at the crash site. (Photo by Jim Ward)

Fuel Tank Pressure placard still left on this piece of wreckage. (Photo by Jim Ward)

Michael Ward, Jim Ward, and Matt Comisky, relax for a moment after placing the granite marker at the crash site of Ensign Joseph W. Schieche's plane. (Photo by Patty Ward)

Chapter 6

Mid-Air Over the Olympics

By David L. McCurry

As the two U.S. Air Force Northrop F-89H Scorpion aircraft maneuvered over the Olympic Mountains of Washington, State, on a practice scramble, pilot 1st Lieutenant Eugene A. Hambly called the pilot of the second F-89H Scorpion aircraft, 2nd Lt. George L. Deer, and asked him to check the bottom of his aircraft. When Lt. Deer pulled up under Lt. Hambly's aircraft, he failed to advise him of this action. 1st Lt. Jim B. Paschall, acting as Lt. Deer's Radar Operator, advised Lt. Deer that he was getting too close, overshooting, and pulling up at the same time. Certain that the two F-89s would contact each other, Lt. Paschall then ducked down a bit. Lt. Deer's F-89 aircraft collided with Lt. Hambly's hitting the left wing and fuselage causing Lt. Deer's aircraft to pitch into a violent nose down attitude.

A very loud noise erupted as the canopy of Lt. Deer's aircraft was released and Paschall was unable to see after that, but felt the aircraft pitch forward at the time he ejected. Following the ejection, Paschall found himself spinning around the longitudinal axis of his body. The horizon lazily passed in and out of view as the earth spun rapidly by. He then flung both arms and legs as far away from his body as possible and then the rotation stopped.

As the horizon passed slowly into view with Paschall situated in a position that appeared proper to pull the dangling rip cord located directly in front of his face; he pulled it. Opening shock at approximately 22,000 feet was mild to nonexistent. The collision, ejection, and wild ride before the parachute opening was terrifying but Lt. Paschall stated that at no time did he loose his sense of training and actions.

As he landed high in the Olympic Mountains of Northwestern Washington, State, Lt. Paschall's parachute began hanging on tree limbs safely lowering him to the ground. It was forty-two hours later when he hiked out of the mountains into civilization.

Lieutenants Deer and Hamby had safely ejected from their two crippled F-89s and were retrieved by helicopters the following day, but radar operator Lt. Robert L. Canup, being unable to operate his ejection system which was torqued after the mid-air collision, died in the crash of his aircraft. The two F-89s had crashed three miles apart on the southeast side of Mt. Olympus, Washington, both disintegrating on impact.

History of the Flight

At 1750 PWT on October 4, 1956 a flight of two Northrop F-89H Scorpion fighter aircraft, serial numbers 54-293, and 54-313, departed Paine Field Air Force Base, Washington, on a tactical action practice scramble. They were both assigned to the 326th Fighter Group, 321st Fighter Interceptor Squadron, at Paine Field.

Lt. Deer's aircraft No. 54-313, call sign "Rammer Baker One," and Lt. Hambly's aircraft No. 54-293, with call sign "Rammer Baker Two" had previously been serviced with the appropriate amount of jet fuel and given their clearances. The Air Route Traffic Control (ARTC) clearance given the pilots of this flight was to climb on a 300 degree heading to an altitude of 1,000 feet on top. The flight to 1,000 feet on top was made under Visual Flight Rules (VFR) conditions. Upon reaching 1,000 feet of altitude, the pilots established contact with "Household Control" located in Blaine, Washington.

The controller at Household advised pilots of "Rammer Baker" one and two to fly a 270 degree heading and contact "Nora Control" located at Neah Bay, Washington. This was the last transmission given at 1759 PWT that Household had made to the Rammer Baker flight. Contact was made between Nora Control and the Rammer Baker flight at 1800 PWT.

Communications with the Rammer Baker flight through Nora Control went as follows: "Rammer Baker flight what is your approximate position and heading?" A response was received from "Rammer Baker One" indicating that they were twenty miles northeast of Port Townsend, on a heading of 270 degrees. Nora Control then asked Rammer Baker One for a pilot's weather report and was advised by the pilot that the flight was climbing VFR with scattered to broken clouds above. At this time there was no painting of the flight on the controller's radar scope with the exception of a blip near the aircraft's supposed location. For the purpose of a more positive identification, the controller decided to give an identification turn to 180 degrees. This turn was observed by a surveillance radar operator at Nora as having been made.

The Nora controller received his first radar contact with the flight at 1810 PWT. Before the controller could make another transmission to the Rammer Baker Flight, he heard the following Rammer Baker flight transmission. "Baker Two, Baker One, what is your position?" "Baker Two in trail, one mile with a visual, over." Rammer Baker One then responded: "Rammer Baker Two, come up and have a look under my aircraft, over." Rammer Baker Two then responded: "Roger." Soon after this transmission was heard, the controller requested Rammer Baker One to squawk two on his transponder. No answer was received and at this time radar contact was lost. Repeated transmissions received no response from the flight. Household control was advised that Nora had lost both radar and radio contact with the Rammer Baker flight at 1812 PWT.

Mercury Control at McChord Air Force Base was advised of the lost contact and was requested to call on all radio control channels in hopes of a response from the Rammer Baker flight. Repeated calls from all of the controllers brought no response. The U.S. Coast Guard at Port Angeles, Washington and Household Control were immediately notified and a search was begun in the area of last contact, 108 degrees and 32 nautical miles from Nora Control. Both aircraft were located on October 7, 1956 and both were completely destroyed.

F-89H: CRASH SITES TODAY

Today the crash sites of the two Northrop F-89H Scorpions, serial numbers 54-313 and 54-293, have been mostly cleaned up other than debris fields of mostly small parts. On the southeast side of Mt. Olympus and just below the Humes Glacier, there are scattered bits of debris on a steep talus slope with small bits of plane parts scattered over a large area down the slope. Most of the larger pieces were hauled out after the accident with the exception of some wing or stabilizer skins and the bottom portion of a vertical stabilizer. As you walk down the slope looking around, you can see bits of aluminum sticking up in random locations with plants growing around the parts. The views around the area are spectacular and even though some argue about litter in this pristine setting, it might be important to leave what is still there as a reminder of our past history.

One of Northrop's retired examples of an F-89J Scorpion at the National Museum of the United States Air Force in Dayton, Ohio. The F-89, an all-weather fighter interceptor, could locate intercept and destroy enemy aircraft by day or night under all types of weather conditions. The first F-89 made its initial flight in August 1948, and the Air Force took deliveries starting in July 1950. Northrop produced a total of 1,050 F-89s for the Air Force. (U.S. Air Force photo)

Spectacular view looking up the Humes Glacier in the Olympic Mountains of Washington, State. One of the two F-89 wrecks is located a few hundred feet lower down the drainage in the talus. (Photo by Scott Waeschle)

Crumpled pieces of aircraft skins like the one pictured can be found throughout the crash site with plants growing around them. (Photo by Scott Waeschle)

View heading to the wreck debris site just down slope from the small snow patch the first hiker is standing on. Walking through the gap and trending left downhill, you will find plane bits scattered everywhere. (Photo by Scott Waeschle)

Aircraft skin from the wrecked F-89 appears to have come from either the rudder or the horizontal stabilizer. (Photo by Scott Waeschle)

Bottom portion of the F-89's rudder with "Do Not Move Rudder Manually" printed on it. (Photo by Scott Waeschle)

Chapter 7

General Aviation and Unidentified Sites

By David L. McCurry

GENERAL Aviation (GA) includes all non-scheduled civil flying, both private and commercial. General Aviation may include business aviation flights, air charter, private aviation, flight training, helicopters, gyrocopters, ballooning, parachuting, gliders, hang gliding, ultralight aircraft, aerial photography, paragliders, foot-launched powered hang gliders, air ambulance, crop dusting, charter flights, aerial traffic reporting, police air patrols, and forest fire fighting air tankers. These are examples but do not include all of General Aviation.

General Aviation got its start basically with the invention of powered flight and the introduction of the Wright Brothers "Wright Flyer" in 1903. There have been literally thousands of General Aviation accidents throughout the Pacific Northwest Region but today, most of the wrecks, old and new, have been cleaned up.

Prior to 1960 there were many old wrecks to be found mainly in mountainous areas, but regulations now require most of the accessible GA wrecks to be removed making these sites now only listings. Today federal agencies such as the Bureau of Land Management, the United States Forest Service, and state laws require insurance companies to remove aircraft wreckage as soon as the investigations have been completed. This is fairly easily done by the use of helicopters.

A large-scale environmental preservation organization operating throughout the United States called "The Sierra Club" has and still is removing old aircraft wrecks of all kinds from environmentally sensitive areas. Their stated mission is "To explore, enjoy, and protect the wild places of the earth, and to enlist and educate humanity to protect and restore the quality of the natural and human environment." Some of the older historically significant aircraft wrecks may seem to some as an eyesore or trash polluting the land, but that presents a controversial issue considering the historic value of rare items, and the fifty-year antiquities protection laws. Unfortunately some take it upon themselves to remove an important old wreck with the attitude that if no one sees who removed the wreck, no one will ever know. It would at least be nice to elect a responsible group to dispose of historic aircraft wrecks in a responsible way.

GA CRASH SITES TODAY

Some of the existing GA wrecks are located in extremely primitive isolated areas such as high rugged mountainous terrain and glaciered mountain tops making them too risky and dangerous for any attempts to remove them. If the risks are too high, they will probably stay there permanently. There are also a few older existing GA wrecks located on private lands. Older GA aircraft wrecks are sometimes very hard to identify because many of the records have been lost, some of the records of registration numbers and accident dates have been mixed up, and in a lot of cases, some of the registration numbers on old aircraft wrecks are either missing or have faded off. With older fabric covered aircraft, because of time and the elements, you will often find only the steel tube frames remaining at crash sites. If the data plate still exists, then we can at least tell what type of aircraft it was.

In some instances we find only parts such as an engine, landing gear, cowling, propeller, or maybe even something like a single wing. It is sometimes fairly difficult to tell exactly what type of aircraft these parts came from, but we can usually identify it as either being GA or a military plane. The same engines and propellers can be used on a variety of different aircraft, but because of the locations of where we found them, we can usually narrow it down to a few possibilities.

Remains of a 300 horsepower Jacobs R-755 radial engine at the crash site of a Cessna C-195 located north of Troy, Oregon. (Photo by Dave McCurry)

Vicki McCurry stands alongside the Jacobs engine at the C-195 crash site. (Photo by Dave McCurry)

Dave McCurry standing on the side of a mountain north of Troy, Oregon, examining the C-195 crash site. (Photo by Vicki McCurry)

Remains of one of the C-195's wings. (Photo by Dave McCurry)

Radial engine found sitting alone in the Cascade Mountains of Washington, State, near Devil's Peak, appears to be a 1,200 horsepower Wright R-1830 Cyclone probably coming from a Grumman F4F Wildcat. (Photo by Andy Dewey)

Bent propeller tips on the Devil's Peak radial engine shows that it probably crashed near there, but there was no wreckage found in the area. (Photo by Andy Dewey)

Unidentified General Aviation wreck found high in the rocks on the south side of Snoqualamie Mountain, Washington. (Photo by Jared Swisher)

Another view of the unidentified Snoqualamie Mountain wreck. (Photo by Jared Swisher)

Wing from Mooney M-20C, N9746M, which crashed at an elevation of 6,705 feet on Mt. Hood, Oregon. Crash date was December 1, 1975. (McCurry collection)

Crash debris from the Mooney aircraft found lying in the rocks can be seen on both sides of the photo. (McCurry collection)

Cockpit and empennage from the crashed Mooney M-20C on Mt. Hood showing part of the broken windscreen, seat frames, left wing, and part of the registration number. (McCurry collection)

Don Hinton and Dave McCurry examine the wreck of a Stinson 108 Voyager found north of Touchet, Washington. This aircraft, apparently returning from a flight to Alaska, crashed on a windy dark night in 1957. (Photo by Vicki McCurry)

Six-cylinder 165 horsepower Franklin engine from the Stinson Voyager wreck. (Photo by Dave McCurry)

Vicki McCurry and Don Hinton examining the Stinson Voyager wreck located in the bottom of a gully created by water run-off. Part of the wreck was buried in mud. (Photo by Dave McCurry)

Chapter 8

"Dutch Roll" Sheds Engines From Boeing 707 Jetliner

By David L. McCurry

WITNESSES living near Oso, Washington, were shocked when on October 19, 1959, they saw a crippled Boeing 707 jetliner smash through trees and crash into the North Fork of the Stillaguamish River. The Braniff International Airways jetliner had been on a test flight over Snohomish County when the accident occurred, killing four of the eight occupants on board.

When residents of the area arrived at the scene, they found that the nose section and wings of the jet were sliced off and the fuselage was flipped over at a right angle to the river. Four survivors of the crash were then seen wading through waist-deep water of the Stillaguamish River looking for other possible survivors.

A report released by the Civil Aeronautics Board stated that a Boeing Airplane Company test pilot was acting as an instructor-pilot on a demonstration and acceptance flight prior to the Boeing 707-227, N7071, being delivered to Braniff Airways. The company was also utilizing this flight time for flight instruction purposes in qualifying airline personnel in the aircraft.

N7071 was a new model of the 707 series aircraft on which FAA type certification flight tests had just been completed. Final certification was awaiting verification of these test results and the aircraft meanwhile was being operated on an experimental certificate of airworthiness. The flight of October 19, 1959, was one of a series of flights to demonstrate to the purchaser that the aircraft met the performance qualities guaranteed by the manufacturer, and to train the Braniff pilots.

The instructor-pilot demonstrated several maneuvers including Dutch Rolls to a pilot-trainee, an airline captain who was making his first training flight prior to a checkout in the Boeing 707.

The instructor-pilot initiated a "Dutch Roll" in which the roll-bank angle of the aircraft reached 40 to 50 degrees. This bank angle was in excess of limitations set by the company for a demonstration of this maneuver. The pilot-trainee, who was to make the recovery, rolled in full right aileron control while the right bank was still increasing. The aircraft immediately yawed and rolled violently to the right. The instructor-pilot then immediately rolled in full opposite aileron and the 707 stopped its right roll at a point well past a vertical bank and then rolled to the left even more violently. Several gyrations followed and after control of the aircraft was regained, it was determined that three of the four engines had separated from the aircraft and it was on fire. The fire rapidly reduced the controllability of the aircraft and an emergency landing was attempted. On the landing attempt, the 707 aircraft struck trees and crashed short of the intended landing area because power on the remaining engine had to be shut down to keep the aircraft wings level.

The flight personnel whom all perished in this accident included Boeing Test Pilot Russell H. Baum, who was fully qualified as an instructor-pilot; Captain John A. Berke, Braniff Airways; Captain M. Frank Staley, Braniff Airways; and George C. Hagan, a Flight Engineer for Boeing. The four personnel who had survived the crash included A.C. Krause, Braniff Airways Flight Engineer; F.W. Symmank, Braniff Airways Technical Instructor; William J. Allsopp, Boeing Aircraft Company Pilot; and W.H. Huebner, an FAA Air Carrier Operations Inspector.

HISTORY OF THE FLIGHT

Shortly before departure, the IFR flight plan which had been filed earlier was cancelled and the flight proceeded according to VFR (visual flight rules) for an estimated four-hour and fifteen-minute flight. Captain Berke, who was making his first flight in the Boeing 707, occupied the left seat and Mr. Baum the right. Mr. Krause was performing the duties of Flight Engineer.

After takeoff from Renton, Washington, and leveling off at an altitude of 12,000 feet, the flight proceeded normally through a series of maneuvers which were first demonstrated by Mr. Baum and then executed by Captain Berke. Several Dutch Rolls in a clean configuration were initiated and the proper recovery was demonstrated by Baum. Captain Berke then made several recoveries from Dutch Rolls in this configuration.

The Dutch Roll characteristic is present in all large aircraft but is more pronounced in those with swept-back wings like the 707. It is most likely to be encountered during approach to landing when the aircraft is at slow speed with a high coefficient of lift and in rough or turbulent air.

Following this, the Boeing 707 was slowed to 155 knots airspeed and 40 degrees of flaps were deployed. Captain Berke then made recoveries from a series of Dutch Rolls in this configuration which were initiated by Mr. Baum. During these rolls, angles of bank greater than 25 degrees were permitted to develop. Mr. Allsopp stated that he leaned over to Mr. Baum and reminded him of the bank-angle restriction. Baum then indicated that he was aware of the restriction. Baum then initiated another Dutch Roll in which the angle of bank was quite large.

Survivors estimated the aircraft rolled 40 to 60 degrees and before attempting recovery, Berke allowed the aircraft to complete several oscillations each of which the roll-bank angle reached 40 to 60 degrees. The Boeing Aircraft Company 707 training manual restricts the Dutch Roll maneuver to a desired maximum roll-bank angle of 15 degrees and an absolute maximum of 25 degrees.

The survivors stated that Berke initiated a recovery while the right bank was still increasing but prior to that, he had applied full right aileron control while the right wing was still moving downward. The airplane yawed heavily to the right and rolled rapidly to the right, well beyond a 90-degree bank.

Immediately after Berke had applied right aileron and early in the yaw-roll movement of the aircraft; Baum took over the controls and applied full left aileron. At that time the aircraft was still rolling to the right. The roll stopped after the wings had passed the vertical and then rolled back to the left even more rapidly and violently than to the right.

The survivors stated that during these two rotations, sounds were heard which could have been the engines separating from the 707 aircraft. They also stated that during these rolls, the thrust levers were seen to snap and the cables go slack.

The movements of the aircraft which followed were described as "spins" or "snap rolls." Although the exact number of rotations could not be determined; the survivors were in agreement that the aircraft rotated to the left and that the rate of roll finally slowed to nearly a stop with the aircraft in an inverted nose down attitude. The left roll was continued and the recovery was made to an upright position with the aircraft in a medium dive.

A normal pullout was made from the dive during which it was noted that the engine instruments indicated a complete absence of thrust on engine numbers 1, 2, and 4. In addition, the thrust levers and start levers for engine numbers 1, 2, and 4 were completely slack. Flight Engineer Krause also reported a complete loss of electrical power.

During most of the flight and throughout the uncontrollable gyrations of the Boeing 707, all eight occupants were on the flight deck. Immediately after control was gained, Mr. Huebner went aft to determine what types of damage had been sustained. He stated that number 1 and 4 engines were gone and there were small fires in the areas where the engines had been attached. He said the number 2 engine was also on fire and it appeared that the forward mount had failed and the engine was hanging down at an angle with the tailpipe pointed into the flap. Huebner then informed the flight deck of his observations.

Shortly after Huebner's report; Mr. Allsopp stated that he saw a very large fire burning in the attachment area of the number 2 engine, and that engine as well as numbers 1 and 4 were all three gone. The aircraft by this time had descended through an overcast and he suggested that an immediate ditching be made in Lake Cavenaugh, which was very close. Baum, who had taken over the controls at the first upset, was apparently looking for a more suitable landing area or attempting to reach an airfield nearby and continued his circle east of the lake.

During this time Mr. Hagan took over the flight engineer's station. The four survivors – Krause, Symmank, Allsopp, and Huebner, then took ditching positions in the rear of the aircraft. The fire emanating from the area of the number 2 engine continued to burn fiercely. It was seen to burn a hole in the flaps and to consume most of the left inboard aileron. It also burned through the top wing surface and the survivors stated that they could see the interior structure of the wing.

Several witnesses located west of the crash site reported hearing booming and whistling sounds as the aircraft travelled on an easterly heading above the overcast. Moments afterward, they described seeing three of the aircraft's engines fall out of the overcast shortly before the jetliner emerged from the clouds on fire.

Mr. Baum had selected a large open field on an attempt for a safe forced landing, but with Flight Engineer Hagen unable to raise the flaps, the jetliner fell short contacting tree tops one-half mile short of the field, and then crashed in the Stillaguamish River bed.

The Boeing 707 first contacted trees wings level at a height of 110 feet on the north side of the river then struck another row of trees at a height of about 90 feet.

A 16 foot long section of the left wing was severed after contacting the trees causing the aircraft to roll left side down. The remains of the left wing then contacted the ground causing several long ditches in the sandy soil just prior to the fuselage striking the ground.

The forward section of the fuselage was completely destroyed by the impact and intense fire which followed killing the four crew members that were seated there. Although badly damaged, the aft section of the fuselage where the survivors were located broke off just to the rear of the trailing edge of the wing and skidded out into the middle of the river. The aft fuselage stayed intact and was not subjected to the ground fire which consumed most of the other wreckage.

INVESTIGATION CONCLUSIONS

The violent gyrations of N7071 which followed the improper Dutch Roll recovery attempt resulted in the separation of the three engines and the inflight fire. A safety factor is designed into the nacelle supporting structure so that in the event of an abnormal landing, it will fail before destructive loads are transmitted to the aircraft's wing. Separation of engines from the aircraft is therefore expected when the aircraft is subjected to high abnormal loadings such as occurred in this case. It was also clear that the Dutch Rolls being performed reached bank angles far in excess of the limitations established by the company. Responsibility for the safety of this aircraft rested solely on the instructor-pilot.

The severity of the gyrations to which the aircraft was subjected to, developed loads greater than the design strength of the nacelle pylon structure. After the three engines were lost and while the flaps were still extended to 40 degrees, the aircraft was committed to land. It was possible that in this configuration, with power available from the number 3 engine, the aircraft could have been flown at least long enough to reach a suitable airport for a crash landing. However, the intense fire which was believed to have come from a ruptured fuel line was threatening the left wing structure, and made an immediate forced landing mandatory.

As the fire gradually destroyed the inboard left aileron and the flight control components in that area, the outboard aileron control was lost. Loss of electrical power cut out the auxiliary hydraulic system which operates the inboard spoilers and the rudder boost. When the left inboard aileron was consumed, the only lateral control remaining to keep the heavily damaged left wing up came from the right inboard aileron and possibly the right outboard spoilers. Lift on the left wing was seriously impaired because of the loss of approximately 35 square feet of upper surface which was burned through, the additional fire damage to the flaps which reduced their effectiveness, the extra drag from the number 2 pylon stub, and the spoiler effect on the upper wing surface caused by the ruptured skin over the fuel vent channels. This drag, coupled with any appreciable thrust from the number 3 engine, would force the left wing down. With limited aileron control available, considerable right rudder would be required to induce a yaw to the right to assist in holding the wing up. However, with the rudder boost inoperative, there would not be sufficient rudder control available to induce enough yaw to counteract these forces. It was then apparent that the number 3 engine was shut down prior to impact so as to be able to keep the wings level with the minimum amount of control available.

After contacting trees and having 16 feet of the left wing severed, control was insufficient to keep the wings level, causing the Boeing 707 jetliner to roll rapidly to the left at a bank angle of approximately 55 degrees before crashing onto the river bank.

The accident investigation board concluded that the accident was the result of the structural failure of the numbers 1, 2, and 4 nacelle pylons, and the fire in the area where the number 2 nacelle broke off. It also concluded that the nacelles failed as a result of overloads imposed on them during several violent uncontrolled gyrations which were encountered when the pilot-trainee applied improper control movement in an attempt to recover from a Dutch Roll.

The board also concluded that the instructor-pilot initiated the Dutch Roll to an angle of bank far in excess of the limitations imposed by the company. In addition, the instructor-pilot was fully aware of these limitations and was reminded of them during this flight. Even knowing that, he permitted the pilot-trainee, who was on his first training flight, to attempt recoveries from these extreme maneuvers.

On conclusion of the accident investigation, the company revised its training syllabus to reduce the possibility of recurrence of a similar type of accident. In addition, the Dutch Roll familiarization was delayed so that the pilot-trainee would have more experience in the aircraft prior to attempting the maneuver.

The company also incorporated a full-time boosted rudder system in the aircraft and increased the vertical stabilizer area and also added a ventral fin. These changes were anticipated to substantially increase the low speed control characteristics of the Boeing 707 aircraft.

BOEING 707: CRASH SITE TODAY

The crash site of N7071 is now in the middle of the Stillaguamish River as the southern bank has eroded probably over 100 feet. On a visit made by Sam Parker in February of 2010, the river was running at near flood levels and no parts of the plane were found. The land owner does find parts on rare occasions, and it's only when the river decides to reveal them. The changing river bank has caused a land feud of sorts among the land owners on the south bank as property lines and markers have been disrupted or destroyed. With the forest floor being covered with several inches of dead leaves and tree branches, combined with erosion and water action, it appears as though all signs of the crash have disappeared.

On October 19, 1959, N7071 a Boeing "Flight Test 707" aircraft in the Braniff Airways livery shown, crashed in the Stillaguamish River about 12 miles northeast of Arlington, Washington. Four of the eight occupants were killed and four others received moderate to serious injuries. (Sam Parker collection)

Investigators in this 1959 photo probe the remains of the Boeing 707 jetliner, N7071, as it lies strewn across the banks of the Stillaguamish River. (McCurry collection)

The fuselage of N7071 as it was seen lying on its left side in the shallow river. (McCurry collection)

Snohomish County Sheriff's deputies investigate the burned out forward fuselage section of the 707 aircraft in which four of its crew members had died. (McCurry collection)

An old photo of the Stillaguamish River as it was in 1989, the earliest available on Google Earth. Note closely the shape of the river, the large sandy southern embankment, and the trees on the northeast side of the river. In 1959, the Braniff Airways Boeing 707 struck these trees and crashed on the sandy embankment. (Google Earth)

Today the current Google Earth photo shows that the sandy embankment is completely gone and is now 15 feet under water. The entire southern embankment has eroded about 100 feet further south and now the crash site is underwater. The large sandbar as seen in this photo was completely underwater during a visit by Sam Parker in late February 2010. (Google Earth)

This is not the river but a small secondary streambed that fills with water when the river floods. A hike of a couple of hundred yards up this streambed is required to get to the Boeing 707 crash site. (Photo by Sam Parker)

Looking west down river, note that the entire southern embankment has been eroded away from past flooding of the river. (Photo by Sam Parker)

This is the group of trees that the Boeing 707 had struck. Although no damage could be seen to the tops, perhaps the trees to the right that are all the same height are the ones that were hit. (Photo by Sam Parker)

After walking more than fifty feet on both sides of the secondary streambed in hopes of finding some kind of evidence, the forest floor was found to be covered with several inches of dead leaves from the trees ending any hopes of finding any small piece of wreckage. All signs of the crash have disappeared due to erosion and water action. The land owner rarely finds parts, and it's only when the river decides to reveal them. (Photo by Sam Parker)

Chapter 9

"Firewood One"

By David L. McCurry

DURING a mountain rescue attempt conducted on September 11, 1980, in the Mt. Redoubt area of the North Cascades Mountains of Washington State, five crew members from Whidbey Island Naval Air Station lost their lives in the crash of a SAR Boeing Vertol CH-46 Sea Knight helicopter, "Firewood One." Two others on board the helicopter survived with serious injuries.

As the helo passed over a ridge it suddenly encountered a strong tailwind causing it to be pushed into a cloud bank. While maneuvering in the clouds and trying to find a clearing, the tandem-rotor CH-46 crashed into Mt. Challenger and burst into flames. The crash occurred only a few months after the Navy search and rescue group based at Whidbey Island Naval Air Station, near Oak Harbor, Washington, had topped the 10,000 hour mark of accident-free flying.

Killed in the crash were: LCDR Dan Mahoney (Pilot); ADC Thomas Sanders (Crew Chief); AMS3 Richard Kubal (Swimmer); LT Patrick Kidgell (Navy Nurse); and HMC Roy Lewis (Corpsman). LT Rick Wall (Copilot) and Dustin Hurlburt (Sheriff's Deputy) survived the crash though badly injured.

Before the crash, everyone knew about the risks, but now all had a gut response to exactly what those risks entailed. It was a sobering experience because the ones who died worked shoulder to shoulder with the rest of the Whidbey rescue group every day. They're gone, but at the same time you realize they were doing exactly what they wanted to do, and if they came back tomorrow, they'd probably be right back up there on another mission.

Tom Townsend, along with a friend, had been mountain climbing in the Mt. Challenger area on the same date of the accident and stumbled onto the crash site by accident. After being so deeply involved in this terrible tragedy; Tom was able to state this account of what he and his hiking friend had witnessed on that day.

In the fall of 1980 my buddy Doug Larsen and I had a few weeks off between our summer jobs as nurse assistants in the burn unit at Harborview Medical Center and college, so we undertook a multiple day trip into the Northern Pickets. With only the "Becky Description" to guide us, we took three days to hike from the Hannagan trailhead to Whatcom Pass and traverse the Whatcom Glacier to Perfect Pass. Our intent was to climb Mt. Challenger and perhaps visit Luna Lake before returning by the same route. We spent the night of September 10, on the Challenger Glacier with hopes of summiting the next day. The weather turned stormy that night and we awoke to white out snow conditions and choose to retrace our tracks and take 2-3 days to hike back to the car. In less than an hour, we found ourselves descending the talus above Perfect Pass at mid-morning and in the fog. We were soon overcome by the distinct smell of aviation fuel and began to see cables and aluminum parts that clearly came from an aircraft. Because we had been through this area less than a day before; we knew an aircraft of some sort had crashed within the last eighteen hours. "Someone goofed up" I recall my then 20 year old mouth saying callously. Within a minute we came upon two victims, both blackened and encased in full flight gear. The corpses were stiff and appeared randomly tossed onto the talus. Our time working in the burn unit had introduced us and in some way hardened us to the injuries these men had. But seeing this, not in a hospital, but in a pristine alpine setting, was shocking and disturbing. As we walked down the rocky slope, our conversation or perhaps the sound of the boulders moving beneath our feet provoked the screams of a survivor. The voice came from under an overturned life raft some 50 feet away. Under the raft was Whatcom County Sheriff's Deputy Dustin Hurlburt, thirsty, hypothermic, and in pain from burns and other injuries. He told us that he had heard another survivor not far away and Doug soon discovered the copilot, Rick Wall, lying on the rocks in full fight gear. His first request was to move his helmet which had slid down over his eyes. He was unable to do this himself because both of his arms were injured. Strapped to his chest was a hand activated (ELT) emergency locator beacon/radio which he was unable to reach (we later learned both arms were broken). I sent out a few maydays and then set it to transmit.

We learned from the survivors that they were part of a seven man naval search and rescue crew which flew the CH-46 out of Whidbey Island. It had the bizarre call name of "Firewood One." The double-rotor helicopter was en route on the evening before, to rescue an injured climber on Mt. Redoubt about ten miles to the north. They apparently flew up the wrong drainage, into a cloud, and crashed where we found them. After discussing the situation with Deputy Hurlburt, we determined that the only sure way to get these men off the mountain was to hike out as quickly as we could to inform the authorities of their location. Because of the poor weather and the fact that they went down far south of their expected course, we suspected that a search from the air would likely take days to find the crash site. These men needed immediate care that we couldn't provide.

Doug and I packed our summit packs, bundled the survivors as best we could, and hiked as quickly as possible the eighteen miles to the trailhead. On the return we opted to traverse below the East Whatcom hanging glacier in an attempt to save time. When we first came across the glacier, it had taken us most of the afternoon navigating around crevasses and lots of other hazards. These were extra precious hours that we did not have for this return trip. We avoided roping up across a glacier by traversing below it. This saved us time but put us in a bowling alley of boulder sized chunks of ice that we had to dodge. A few blocks came down, but none near us. Doug recalls jogging the one-half mile or so on glacier polished rock, always looking up to see if I could detect any motion above us or ahead of us that could put us in harm's way. We were lucky that no big chunks of ice calved off the glacier that day. We arrived after dark, tired as hell to a hero's welcome at the camp of a volunteer rescue group set up to aid in the effort to find the missing helicopter.

We then arrived at the trailhead after midnight, extremely tired and expecting to drive down the mountain to get help. We found volunteer rescue crews bustling with activity at the trail head, but with no place to go, because the missing helicopter had not been located. When we had activated the Emergency Locator Transmitter at the crash site, the signal began bouncing off the peaks throughout the area which had sent confusing signals to the authorities. At least one good signal had been received, so the rescue crews hoped that the crash site could soon be located. The first group that we met with gave us a "look-over" as just more hikers. We asked the first guy we had encountered if they had lost a helicopter because of the fact of the crashed one we had just found, and we could have pushed him over with a feather with such a look of shock on his face. The rest was a blur, driving down the mountain to the ranger's headquarters, numerous meetings with the various rescue authorities, confirming the location of the crash site as being Perfect Pass on various maps, and being treated like heroes by everyone involved for finding the lost search and rescue crew.

A break in the weather allowed a Canadian mountain rescue helicopter to hoist Rick and Dustin off the mountain the next day, and both fully recovered and eventually returned to their previous lives. Five men died that day and the crash of Firewood One caused a major change in the way that the Navy conducts civilian search and rescue missions.

FIREWOOD ONE: CRASH SITE TODAY

Twenty years later the date of 9/11 would take on a historic significance and be burned into the national consciousness forever, but for Tom Townsend that day, in 1980, in one of the most remote places in the lower 48, it became a touchstone event. He attended a 25th anniversary ceremony at Naval Air Station Whidbey, and got to talk for the first time with family members of some of the victims and the man who directed the rescue mission. The group watched as a naval SAR helicopter took off to deliver a wreath to the site of the crash.

Two years later he hiked for a second time to Perfect Pass and saw that same wreath, now brown and brittle, at the base of a monument the navy had placed there during the 1980s. The clouds blew through him just like on his previous visit. The alpine travelers who've passed this way have left undisturbed the few bits of remaining wreckage, and they are preserved almost as if the crash happened a week before. Tom wept at the time; perhaps it was the touch of the ghosts of the five men whose lives were consumed in a ball of fire on that spot almost three decades earlier. More likely it was the heart of a 47 year old man, now a husband and father, recalling the brash 20 year old who was lucky enough to be in the right place at the right time 27 years previous.

An original photo of the Navy SAR Boeing Vertol CH-46 Sea Knight helicopter "Firewood One" which was lost during a mountain rescue attempt conducted on September 11, 1980, in the Mt. Redoubt area of the North Cascades Mountains of Washington State. Five crew members from Whidbey Island Naval Air Station lost their lives in the crash of this helicopter which also seriously injured two others. The first U.S. Marine Corps CH-46 was delivered in 1964 and by 1990; Boeing Vertol had delivered over 600 Sea Knights. (Photo by Gary Vincent)

Tom Townsend stands alongside a bronze plaque attached to a large granite boulder at Perfect Pass bearing the names of the five navy airmen whom lost their lives there in the crash of their CH-46 Sea Knight helicopter. (Photo by Tom Townsend)

Broken rear view mirror from "Firewood One" is one of a few bits of remaining wreckage preserved almost as if the crash happened a week before. (Photo by Tom Townsend)

Distant view shows the memorial plaque attached to the large granite boulder. (Photo by Tom Townsend)

Another piece of wreckage remaining at the CH-46 Sea Knight crash site is this engine access panel. (Photo by Tom Townsend)

Close-up view of the memorial plaque placed in memory of the crew of "Firewood One." (Photo by Tom Townsend)

The crash involving "Firewood One" occurred in the fog shrouded mountains near Mt. Challenger at Perfect Pass, one of the most remote places in the lower 48. (Photo by Tom Townsend)

Chapter 10

B-47E Refueling Technique Turns Night Mission Into Disaster

By David L. McCurry

B-47E serial number 51-7042 was scheduled to participate in a 22nd Bombardment Wing mission, which was to include night air refueling in the Utah/Nevada area with a 6,000 pound fuel transfer during a twenty minute contact. A general mission meeting had been conducted at 1530, 17 July 1957, covering specialized and late weather briefings for the training mission which was scheduled for the following night.

The crew for the Boeing Stratojet Bomber consisted of: Maj. Frank A. Henss (Aircraft Commander); 1st Lt. Willaim C. Kuster (Co-Pilot); Capt. Robert E. Craycraft (Observer); and Lt. Albert H. Sarchet (Student Observer).

The forecast weather for the refueling area was briefed as being scattered thunderstorms, turbulence, and lightning. The refueling area was originally briefed to be on a track between Caliente, Nevada and South Currie, Nevada, but a late change for the refueling area had moved the mission downstream 120 miles due to other traffic in the rendezvous area.

According to the USAF Accident Report, B-47E, number 51-7042, departed March Air Force Base, California at 2013 PST, 18 July 1957 as number #3 in a cell of four aircraft with takeoff intervals of one and one-half minutes. Cell join-up was made on climb-out and level-off was completed at 25,000 feet. The portion of the flight from takeoff to the rendezvous area was uneventful. Rendezvous and descent to the refueling altitudes was accomplished as briefed. After the initial contact with the tanker cell was made at 18,500 feet, the tanker cell leader, observing buildups ahead, initiated a climb in an attempt to maintain on-top flight. After leveling off at 19,500 feet, a fuel transfer was started and completed, and the receiver aircraft, B-47E, 51-7042, dropped back to the observation position.

At this time Maj. Henss, the commander of 51-7042, reported that he had a total of 69,500 pounds of fuel on board. While Maj. Henss was in the observation position, the tanker initiated a second climb in order to clear buildups. During the climb, all aircraft in the cell encountered intermittent cloud conditions.

Being real heavy and while trying to maneuver with the slower KC-97 prop tanker plane which was cruising at an airspeed of 165-170 knots; 51-7042 was now keeping pace at approximately the stalling speed for the B-47E. 51-7042 apparently suffered an engine failure on the number #6 engine but it was uncertain when or if this was the initiating event in the following sequence.

After the tanker started to climb, B-47E number 51-7042 was seen passing low and to the right. Approximately two minutes later, a flash was observed at about the tanker's five o'clock position. An immediate radio search was initiated to determine if the flash observed was one of the cell aircraft. All aircraft reported except 51-7042. At this time appropriate ground stations were notified that 51-7042 was missing. Ground witnesses reported an aircraft exploding and crashing in mountainous terrain, eight and one-half miles west of Shafter, Nevada.

Within a matter of minutes, the boom operator of the tanker aircraft noted and called the pilot with regard to a large bright flash of light which illuminated the clouds and lasted for several seconds. This flash was not similar to any report of lightning which was prevalent in the area. The flash was later on established to be the terminal event of the accident.

A rescue team arriving at the crash site of 51-7042, immediately determined that all four airmen had perished in the accident. The aircraft had suffered catastrophic airframe failures and debris from the aircraft was spread out over a two mile wide area. Observer Robert E. Craycraft was the only person who had managed to eject out of the stricken bomber, but his automatic lap belt release had failed to function, along with a failure of the automatic parachute opening device. His body still strapped in the navigator's seat by lap and shoulder harnesses was found approximately 750 yards upstream to the main impact area of the crew compartment.

INVESTIGATION CONCLUSIONS

Accident analysis revealed that the landing gear

was extended, and the flaps were full down. It was determined by the investigation committee that the aircraft commander of 51-7042 lowered full flaps in order to maintain cell position at low airspeeds. Then due to lightning, turbulence, and thunderstorm activity, accompanied by the failure of the number #6 engine, the aircraft went into an unusual attitude. During an attempted recovery, the aircraft assumed excessive airspeed and the landing gear was lowered as a braking device. During the pull-out, the B-47E broke apart and fell onto the Pequop Mountains near Shafter, Nevada.

The fallout pattern of debris indicated structural failures of the wings, engine pylons, and fuselage prior to impact into the mountains. The breakup was shown to be due to excessive load factors applied during the attempted recovery, in all probability when the aircraft commander visualized his altitude above the terrain and attempted a pull-out.

A possible contributing factor to the accident was the cell leader being preoccupied with instructing a student in his aircraft on refueling techniques and not maintaining normal cell control during hazardous operating conditions. Adding to this terrible tragedy was the possibility of a structural weakness in the wing structures of the B-47 type aircraft.

Author's Note

Investigations of other B-47 accidents during the following year revealed a design flaw and weakness in wing structures of these type aircraft. Conclusive evidence that a structural crisis had been reached came on 13 March 1958 when two B-47s broke up in midair in separate incidents. Near Homestead Air Force Base, Florida, a B-47B disintegrated after its center wing section failed at 15,000 feet, three minutes after takeoff. The aircraft had a total flight time of 2,077 hours and thirty minutes at the time of the accident. The same day a TB-47B broke up at 23,000 feet over Tulsa, Oklahoma, after the bottom skin plate of the left wing failed causing the left wing to break off at the same point. This plane had flown a total of 2,418 hours and 45 minutes. While Air Force and contractor agencies were investigating these two accidents, three more occurred, indicating that the crashes of 13 March were not isolated events.

These successive accidents further served notice that the flaws might show up in almost any B-47, not just those with over 2,000 flight hours. On 21 March, as a result of over stress from a pull-up, a B-47E disintegrated in midair near Avon Park, Florida. This aircraft had a total flight time of only 1,129 hours and 30 minutes. Next, a B-47E seemed to explode at 13,100 feet just prior to a refueling rendezvous near Langford, New York, on 10 April. This aircraft had a total flight time of 1,265 hours and 30 minutes. The final tragedy in this series occurred on 15 April 1958 when another B-47E, with a total flight time of 1,419 hours and 20 minutes, took off into a storm from MacDill Air Force Base, Florida, and disintegrated shortly afterwards. The pilot was believed to have encountered wind gusts of 80 to 100 miles per hour. One of these accidents was ascribed to the pilot exceeding the aircraft structural limits in a pull-up, but the remaining four were clearly due to structural fatigue failure.

B-47E, 51-7042: Crash Site Today

This crash site is unique in that two different military aircraft struck this same mountain range twelve years apart and within one mile of each other making it almost appear to some that it was only one crash site. I had made prior arrangements to visit both the General Dynamics F-111A and Boeing B-47E sites in the Pequop Mountains near Shafter, Nevada, with Jason Watt from Boise, Idaho, whom had visited the sites years ago. We had set a date for September of 2014, and by the time we were set to travel, we had recruited a large number of wreck hunters to join with us and visit the two crash sites. Jason was mostly interested in learning more about the sites and the families of the airmen involved, and I was there to do a book story.

The plan was to meet in Wells, Nevada, the evening before, and then at our planned rendezvous point the following morning which was offices for the Newmont Mine Long Canyon Project located twenty-five miles to the east of Wells. At the Newmont Mine offices we met with Newmont geologist Jeff Blackmon who was assigned to lead us through the private Newmont property to an area where we could start our climb on the Pequop Mountain Range to the crash sites.

Our plan was to drive two vehicles to a point as high as we could get to on the 9,249 foot summit. Craig Fuller and his wife Rasa would drive their Toyota Tacoma truck and Jason Watt would drive his Chevrolet van. With those two vehicles they could accommodate our entire wreck hunting group. With a steep climb up a seldom used mountain road, Jason's van had bottomed out several times hitting large rocks imbedded in the center of the road. We made it as far as we figured Jason could drive to, parked his van, and then used Craig's truck to shuttle us to the highest point we could drive to. On reaching the top of the Pequop Mountains, the view was stunning!

Our hike to the first crash site which was the F-

111 would take us two miles south across the mountains to a point above 9,000 feet in altitude where we started to find the first pieces of debris from the crashed F-111. We spent most of the day documenting the F-111 site and discovered to our surprise that most of this aircraft is still on the mountain. It was so interesting that we wound up spending more time there than what we had allotted for.

By the time that our party had all gathered together for our hike down the steep east side of the mountain, it was getting late in the afternoon. Part of our plan was to descend down the mountain to the B-47 crash site and then meet with the two vehicles at the base of the mountain which was approximately a 2,500 foot descent. Rasa Fuller along with Dave Trojan and Jason Watt hiked back across the mountain ridge to retrieve the vehicles and would meet the rest of us at the base of the mountain after we had visited the B-47 site.

The terrain was incredibly steep while traversing down the slope to the B-47 impact crater. On arrival it was late and already starting to get dark. We took a few photos of the impressive crater and then started down a steep canyon which held most of the remains of the B-47E. By the time we reached the bottom of the canyon, none of us had seen any signs of the two vehicles that were supposed to meet us there.

A big mistake that some of us had made was not bringing flash lights. Thankfully Craig had several spares. After reaching the base of the canyon, we still had nearly a two mile hike to a point where several members of our group had planned to camp out. John and Deb Wirt had stationed their vehicle with a flashing red light mounted on the roof to help guide us in the dark to their camp. That was a huge help. It was getting cold and windy and still no sign of the vehicles. We sat on a hill waiting and watching when finally we spotted some headlights far below us and several miles away. It was only one vehicle and we could see that they were clearly lost while trying to find their way around on several intersecting dirt roads. We watched for what seemed like more than thirty minutes until it was obvious that the vehicle was finally headed in our direction. For a while we didn't know if the vehicle was intended for us, but then it became obvious that they were searching for us. When the vehicle pulled up, it was Rasa Fuller and Dave Trojan. They had GPS coordinates for where to meet us, but got confused with the intersecting dirt roads. We asked where Jason Watt was, and then is where a long story got started.

On reaching the two vehicles, Jason discovered that the oil pan on his van had struck a rock, punctured it, and leaked most of the crankcase oil out of it.

Jason was able to start the van and head it down the mountain but that was as far as he could go. Rasa had never towed a vehicle before but had a tow line and the vehicle to tow it with. She ended up having to tow Jason's van all the way down the mountain and near a main gravel road which was a very long way. While Jason tended to his van, Rasa and Dave drove up the mountain to retrieve us. It was late and getting cold so we were very thankful for their arrival.

The following day we drove to Wells where part of our group went to an auto parts store and found some temporary patching material along with some motor oil. After delivering the items to Jason, the rest of us went on hunting for some other crash sites while Jason and Dave Schwarz applied the temporary patch and drove his van back to Boise.

Because of it being dark on arriving to the B-47 crash site, we decided to make a return trip back to the site the following spring to document it in good daylight. We devised a good plan only this time it would be different.

After a lot of phone calls and emails, we had a date set to visit the crash site of B-47E, 51-7042, again in June of 2015. This time our primary mission would be to place a nice memorial monument at the site.

Jason Watt had devised the plan for the monument and had contacted John Craycraft, the son of Robert E. Craycraft, over the winter for his thoughts on building the monument. After discussing where to place the monument and plaque, Jason then sent John an email showing him a rough sketch of the completed memorial. After reviewing what Jason had drawn, John then thought this was a good idea. After agreeing to the idea, Jason mocked it up out of cardboard. After both being sold on the design, Jason then had the steel plate monument base parts cut out on a plasma table by a friend who works at a performance automotive shop. Being a welder by trade; Jason's friend then welded the base of the monument together allowing for Jason to do the finish work. Jason spent considerable time grinding the welds down for the finished product and then got it powder coated in black. Jason also pre-made a wood form that concrete would be poured into to hold the monument base. John designed and supplied a beautiful bronze plaque that would be bolted to the steel base of the monument at the site of the memorial.

Our group met again at 6:30 am with Jeff Blackmon at the Newmont Mine offices to get an early start and try to beat the June heat. Out of his own kindness, Jason supplied a nice meat sandwich lunch with fruit and water for our group. The members of the second group included: Jason Watt; Dave Schwarz; Jeff Blackmon; John Craycraft; Evelyn Craycraft; Joe

Craycraft; Dave and Vicki McCurry; Don Hinton; Dave Trojan; Sam Parker; John Wirt; and Jerry Bowen.

Our trip, led by Jeff Blackmon, through the Newmont mine property to the mouth of the canyon where the monument would be placed, was very uneventful this time. By use of a four-wheeler ATV, Dave Schwarz hauled one hundred pounds of dry concrete in bags up the canyon along with water and a mixing pan for the project. Using stud bolts and epoxy glue, the bronze plaque was then mated to the monument base supplied by Jason. The wood frame was placed on a large rock and supported inside by small crushed rock hauled from the side of the mountain in buckets by our group. A small square wire rebar was then placed into the bottom of the wood frame to steady the base of the monument after the concrete was poured. We then all took turns mixing concrete with shovels and water. After the monument was placed into the concrete filled wood frame, the base of the monument was also filled with concrete through a port in the back side of the base. After using a level to make sure everything was even and square, members of the group then did concrete finishing around the base and wood form of the monument. It took approximately four hours in 95 degree heat to complete this project, and then afterword we had a small celebration with John Craycraft playing the taps on his trumpet. It was a great tribute to those that had lost their lives there.

After completing the placement of the memorial monument, several members of the group then made a trip up the mountain to document parts of the plane. After re-grouping, half of us then travelled to Wendover, Utah to enjoy a barbeque dinner supplied by Jeff Blackmon at his condo.

The Boeing B-47 Stratojet was the world's first swept wing bomber, and was capable of speeds in excess of 600 mph. The B-47E which first flew on 30 January 1953 was powered by six J47-GE-25A turbojet engines, which featured a significant improvement in the form of water-methanol injection. (U.S. Air Force)

Homecoming photo of SAC B-47E crew arriving back from Guam on July 6, 1957. Pictured from left to right: Capt. Robert E. Craycraft and wife Eleanor; Major Frank E. Henss and unidentified woman; unidentified man, (possibly the crew chief); 1st Lt. William C. Kuster and his wife; and another unidentified male. (Photo courtesy of Randy Williams)

It is hard to comprehend the kind of forces that instantly created this crater caused by the crash of the B-47E in the Pequop Mountains of Nevada. (Photo by Dave McCurry)

John Craycraft, (son of Captain Robert E. Craycraft), holds the bronze plaque that he designed and supplied for the memorial monument at the crash site of B-47E, serial number 51-7042. (Photo by Dave Trojan)

United States Air Force photo of Captain Robert E. Craycraft. (Photo courtesy of John Craycraft)

John Craycraft (in blue shirt) watches as members of the group mix water with bags of concrete for the B-47E memorial. (Photo by Dave McCurry)

Jason Watt and Dave Trojan do the finishing work as the concrete for the memorial begins to set-up. (Photo by Dave McCurry)

Data Plate from the B-47E found on a piece of wreckage. (Photo by Dave McCurry)

One of two throttle quadrants found at the crash site. (Photo by Dave McCurry)

Pieces of the B-47's shattered fuselage were found scattered all over the mountain. (Photo by Dave McCurry)

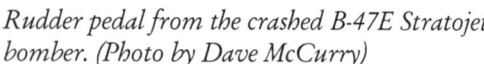

Rudder pedal from the crashed B-47E Stratojet bomber. (Photo by Dave McCurry)

Remains of the B-47's Strategic Air Command badge from the nose of the bomber showing the "C" and "A" in yellow with a red border. (Photo by Don Hinton)

One of the six J-47-GE-25A turbojet engines still remaining at the crash site of B-47E, 51-7042. (Photo by Dave McCurry)

John Craycraft plays the taps on his trumpet for a small group ceremony at the conclusion of the B-47E memorial installation. (Photo by Dave Trojan)

Sunrise view of the completed B-47E memorial in the Pequop Mountains of Nevada. (Photo by Jason Watt)

Chapter 11

"Article 123"
The Cover Up

By David L. McCurry

THE Lockheed A-12, built for the Central Intelligence Agency (CIA) was the fastest, highest flying human piloted jet aircraft in history. The reconnaissance aircraft which was capable of flying at more than three times the speed of sound, and at an altitude of 90,000 feet, was produced in secrecy at Lockheed's "Area 51" Skunk Works and based on the designs of Clarence "Kelly" Johnson. The code name given to the A-12 was Oxcart, a name designation given to the A-12 research and development program by the CIA which was selected from a random list of codenames. The A-12 designation was the 12th in a series of design efforts with the "A" referring to "Archangel", the internal code name for the aircraft. The crews named the A-12 the Cygnus in order to follow Lockheed's practice of naming aircraft after celestial bodies.

The A-12 was produced from 1962 to 1964 and was operational from 1963 until early 1968. It was the precursor to the twin-seat YF-12 prototype interceptor, M-21 drone launcher, and the SR-71 Blackbird. The A-12 was designed to succeed the U-2 spy plane on missions over the Soviet Union and Cuba, but was never used for that role. Instead the A-12s were used over Vietnam photographing missile sites, and during the Pueblo crisis with North Korea.

The first five A-12s produced in 1962 were initially flown with Pratt & Whitney J75 engines capable of producing 17,000 pounds of thrust each, which enabled these A-12s to obtain speeds of approximately Mach 2.0. In 1963 with newly developed J58 engines, the A-12s obtained speeds of Mach 3.2. On the 24th of May 1963, the program lost its first A-12, serial number 60-6926, when "Article 123" piloted by Kenneth S. Collins crashed south of Wendover, Utah.

Article 123 was the third A-12 built and was powered by two J75 engines because of problems associated with the J58 engines at that time. Because of the fact that Article 123 never received the intended J58 engines, it never reached its design speed of Mach 3.0 and was undergoing testing when it crashed.

On its 79th flight with CIA pilot Kenneth Collins at the controls; the A-12 was being flown for subsonic engine testing because of fuel control problems which were plaguing the aircraft during accelerations and cruise flight. Collins had taken off from "Area 51" and was cruising at Mach .85 at an altitude of 34,000 feet over build-ups of cumulus and cirrus clouds near the Utah border when a failure of the pitot system occurred. While entering clouds, Collins noticed erroneous airspeed indications and tried to correct them, but the A-12 nearing stall speed pitched up and entered a flat inverted spin at 30,000 feet. After making several attempts to correct an unrecoverable spin situation, Collins ejected from the A-12 aircraft after passing through 25,000 feet of altitude. Following his safe ejection, Collins watched his ejection seat and the inverted spinning A-12 as it impacted the desert floor fourteen miles south of Wendover, Utah.

The accident investigation revealed that inadequate pitot tube heating had caused moisture that was trapped in the pitot system to freeze which blocked the pitot tube. Collins had engaged the autopilot and tried pitching the aircraft down to gain more airspeed, but the erroneous data caused a stability augmentation system failure which caused the aircraft to pitch up and stall.

THE COVER UP

After safely parachuting to the ground, pilot Ken Collins was greeted by four men who had driven up in a red pickup truck after seeing his parachute come down near U.S. Hwy. 93. Driving over rough gravel roads they had also retrieved the ejection seat which they had thrown in their pickup bed. They offered Collins a ride to the crashed plane, but Collins used a pre-arranged plan and told them it was an F-105 jet fighter and that he needed a ride to Wendover, Nevada, as a cover up story to keep the civilians away from the crash site. After being dropped off at the state police headquarters in Wendover, Collins was able to make a telephone call to the Area 51 base. The base then sent a Lockheed Constellation loaded with security people and aircraft engineers to Wendover in less than two hours. Kelly Johnson, the designer of the aircraft, also arrived at the crash scene. The top secret A-12 had crashed on public land and efforts began immediately to secure the site and recover the wreckage.

In a dramatic effort to cover the secrecy of the crash of Article 123, the CIA called the accident aircraft a Republic F-105 Thunderchief as a cover story. Witnesses and the local law enforcement were warned with "dire consequences" to keep quiet about the crash. Each was paid $25,000 in cash to do so. Cash payments were commonly used to avoid inquiries into its operations, and contracted security guards were paid $1,000 monthly plus given free housing on base.

By daybreak the next day, recovery crews from nearby Hill AFB had already covered all of the remaining large pieces of wreckage with tarps to conceal the identity of the aircraft. Despite objections that it might impede the accident investigators ability to determine the cause, heavy equipment including a bulldozer were brought in to quickly load large pieces of the top secret titanium wreckage onto trucks and erase all evidence of the aircraft. The large center section required being cut up by cutting torches before being loaded aboard a flatbed truck. All of the smaller bits and pieces were meticulously picked up by hand and placed in boxes to be sent to Wendover.

To conceal the final destination of the recovered wreckage, two Douglas C-124 cargo planes were flown to Wendover to load and transport the remains back to Area 51. Within two days the site was considered sanitized.

By creating a cover story to prevent public exposure of the Oxcart program and to keep Area 51 also known as "The Ranch" by most people that worked there a secret, a news story was written claiming that a cloud of secrecy surrounded the crash of a 2.5 million dollar Republic F-105 jet fighter near the Nevada Utah border. The headlines read: "Mystery surrounds jet plane crash." The pilot was not identified but was said to have ejected safely. He was described as being a Hughes Aircraft Company employee and that he was testing some electronics equipment. The F-105 was reported as having been assigned to the Air Research and Development Center at Wright-Patterson Air Force Base located near Dayton, Ohio. By calling the crashed aircraft an F-105, news coverage was guaranteed to be minimal. The U.S. government had to make sure that no traces of the A-12 crash debris might be found and disclosed to adversaries.

ARTICLE 123: A-12, 60-6926: CRASH SITE TODAY

Very little remains today at the crash site of "Article 123" making it difficult to find the site, but there a few identifying features including a road and terrain that finally led our wreck hunting group onto the site. At first glance looking out over the remote Nevada desert, you would never have thought this accident had happened there. The A-12 impact scar is only visible if you know exactly where to look. After walking the site and looking very close you can still find small bits of titanium. Other items that we spotted were a few turbine blades from the engines, pieces of circuit boards, pieces of black honeycomb material, radar-absorbing asbestos and composite materials, and a cockpit warning indicator and button. Craig Fuller brought along his drone aircraft and shot some awesome aerial photos of the impact site that showed marks in the ground made by the A-12's engines and fuselage. Even though the cleanup was very meticulous, it showed us that you can never completely cleanse a site.

Eight Lockheed A-12s and two YF-12s at Groom Lake's "Area 51", circa 1964. (Photo U.S. Government)

The crash site of "Article 123" south of Wendover, Nevada, showing part of the wing center section and engine nacelle. (Photo U.S. Government)

Craig Fuller on the left confirms the crash site of Article 123, while Vicki McCurry on the right walks up the hill to the aircraft's impact area. (Photo by Dave McCurry)

Small pieces of titanium along with radar-absorbing asbestos can still be found around the crash site. (Photo by Dave McCurry)

Tarps were used to cover the larger pieces of wreckage to help conceal the identity of the A-12. (Photo U.S. Government)

Dave McCurry holds a small piece of titanium found at the A-12 crash site. Note the mountains in the background that match the original crash site photo. (Photo by Vicki McCurry)

The largest piece of titanium structure that was found at the crash site. (Photo by Dave McCurry)

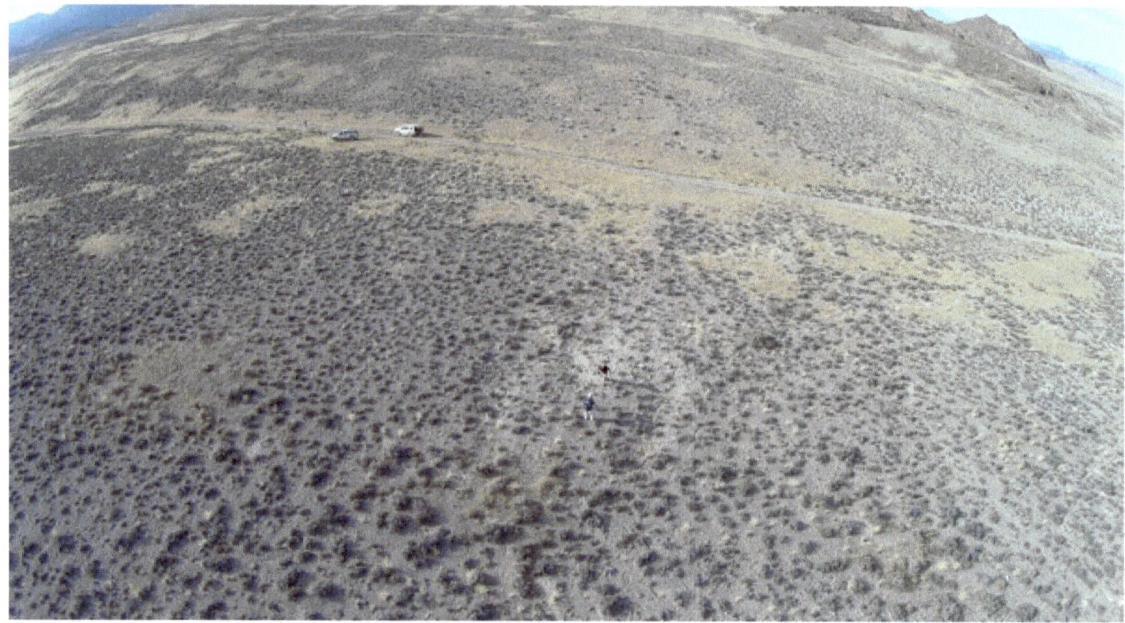

Photo from drone aircraft remotely piloted by Craig Fuller. Don Hinton and Dave McCurry can be seen standing in the crater, left over from the crash of Article 123. Note the marks left in the ground from the impact of the engines and fuselage. (Photo by Craig Fuller)

Small debris left at the crash site including black honeycomb material. (Photo by Dave Trojan)

Other items found at the crash site included engine turbine blades with part numbers, strange green colored objects, a cockpit warning indicator and button, and pieces of electrical circuit boards. (Photo by Dave Trojan)

Dave Trojan holds an unidentifiable part (presumably from the A-12) found at the far north end of the A-12 crash site. (Photo by Dave McCurry)

A thick piece of glass, probably from the aircraft's canopy, was also found on the north end of the crash site. (Photo by Dave McCurry)

Chapter 12

Speed Brakes: A Fatal Consequence To A Sabre Jet Forced Landing

By David L. McCurry

A normal takeoff by Colonel Henry Hudson Norman in his North American F-86H Sabre, serial number 52-2082, from Wendover Air Force Base, Utah, was completed at 0553 local time on 20 August, 1955. He was commander of the 312th Fighter-Bomber Wing and a member of the Wing Gunnery Team competing in the Ninth Air Force Gunnery Match at Wendover AFB, Utah. The flight on this day was an air-to-ground skip bomb and low angle strafe mission involving a flight of four F-86H aircraft and was led by Captain Shelby A. Evans; call sign "Kimball." Weather for the flight was briefed as being 5,500 scattered and 15 miles visibility.

The flight proceeded to the range located 45 miles NE of Wendover AFB and completed the gunnery portion of the mission without incident. After the last pass, members joined up over a predesignated rendezvous point, 35 miles northeast of Wendover at 10,000 feet indicated altitude.

The U. S. Air Force Accident Report stated that Col. Norman was observed by other members of the flight to lag behind during join-up and assumed last position in right echelon. Capt. Evans then set course for Wendover AFB at 10,000 feet of altitude and 260 knots indicated airspeed. Soon thereafter, Col. Norman flying the number #2 position called Capt. Evans and asked him for a fuel reading. Capt. Evans stated that he had 1300 lbs. and #3 had 1200 lbs. Later Col. Norman advised that both inverters on his aircraft were inoperative. Capt. Evans now had 1050 lbs. of fuel and told Col. Norman to check the inverter circuit breakers and switches and that he should now have 850 lbs.

After these transmissions, flight leader Evans called for a change to tower frequency. Immediately following the change of frequency, Col. Norman declared a partial engine flame-out but stated that the engine was operating again. Their altitude remained at 10,000 feet MSL which was approximately 5,750 feet above the terrain, and their distance now was estimated to be approximately 12 miles from Wendover AFB. As Col. Norman slowly dropped back, other members of the flight lost sight of him and promptly initiated a 180 degree turn in an attempt to render assistance. Col. Norman requested the best glide speed in which Capt. Evans responded with it being 195 knots.

Capt. Evans continued a search for Col. Norman who was now stating that the engine was quitting again although some tailpipe temperature remained. Capt. Obranovich in the #3 position descended to within 50 feet above the terrain in an attempt to check its features for a possible forced landing within an area which Col. Norman was thought to be located. Lt. Siran in the #4 position was first to locate Col. Norman and kept him in sight for the remainder of the flight. Lt. Siran then called Wendover tower and requested they clear the pattern for a straight-in forced landing which Col. Norman was attempting. Lt. Siran advised Col. Norman to retract his speed brakes in which Col. Norman replied, "Aren't they in? The switch is in." Capt. Evans advised Col. Norman not to lower his landing gear until he was assured of making a landing on the runway. An air start procedure started by Capt. Evans was discontinued when Col. Norman was two and one-half miles from the runway and 500 feet above the terrain. About this time, Col. Norman radioed that he didn't think he would make the runway.

On his attempt to make a safe forced landing, Col. Norman made a last minute correction to the right, presumably to select a more suitable landing site. Lt. Siran stated that Col. Norman's aircraft touched down in a normal landing attitude with the gear up and speed brakes out. Col. Norman's F-86 aircraft skipped lightly along the top of several small sand dunes before settling down onto a solid skid. When it looked like the landing would be successful, the right wing suddenly struck the bottom portion of a large four foot high sand dune solidly. The fuselage immediately separated from the wings at this point and began tumbling and rolling coming to rest 150 yards from where it hit the dune. It had broken into two parts at the rear of the cockpit floor. The seat tore loose from the floor fatally injuring Col. Norman as it tumbled twenty-four yards to the left and forward of the nose section. The lap belt initiator had also fired releasing Col. Norman's body from the seat.

Parts of the canopy, pilot's visor, and oxygen

mask, along with other parts of the aircraft were found between the dune and main fuselage sections, indicating the fuselage had rolled and tumbled while maintaining the same direction after striking the dune. Col. Norman had apparently died instantly from multiple head injuries. A small fire broke out in the aft fuselage section which was extinguished by crash rescue personnel from Wendover.

ACCIDENT INVESTIGATION AND ANALYSIS

The terrain selected for the forced landing was flat but heavily dotted with small mounds of sand on top of which normally grew scrub brush. The first signs of ground contact were the scrapped tops of small dunes, some with paint from the wings evident. The aircraft didn't settle in with solid ground contact for seventy-five yards after contacting the tops of the sand mounds indicating that it still had flying speed for this distance. Separation of the wing structure and fuselage was obviously caused by impact of the right wing with a large sand mound. This separation eliminated any chance of survival as the fuselage tumbled and rolled with the canopy striking the ground at several points. There was also evidence of the speed brakes still having been extended at the time of ground contact.

Evidence of a sizeable amount of fuel was found in and around the center wing section in which the main fuel cell was located. The soil was moist and soggy with fuel found within a small area adjacent to the cell outlet more than twenty-four hours after the accident. The center wing section was overturned later to permit access to boost pumps within the center wing fuel cell where more fuel poured from the cell outlet. After examining the boost pumps, it was noted that more fuel still remained in the cell. Fuel remaining at the time of the engine flameout was estimated at 800 lbs. based upon the findings and statements of fuel readings furnished by other flight members. This factor eliminated the lack of a supply of fuel as a cause of the flameout. Col. Norman stated that both inverters were inoperative prior to the flameout, but those failures could not have had any connection with the flameout. However, fuel flow and fuel quantity gauges would become inoperative with this type of failure making air starts extremely difficult considering fuel flow is a critical item during air starts.

It appeared that the engine did not flame out instantly. Col. Norman called out that "the engine was going again, and had died again" several times. Therefore it was assumed that the engine surged before complete flameout. Maintenance records revealed a fuel controller change on 19 August, 1955 where an adequate test had been completed prior to the flight. No other maintenance factors were noted that may have contributed to the accident.

The question arose as to why the pilot chose a straight-in approach to Wendover Air Force Base, estimated at 9.9 miles distance, rather than to land gear-up on the salt flats over which the flameout occurred. Other pilots indicated a similar decision would have been made under the same conditions. Each thought the field was within marginal gliding distance. Estimation of glide distance considering altitude available and a clean configuration (landing gear and flaps up) tended to confirm the opinions and the decision of the pilot that the runway could be reached safely for a forced landing. It was also stated by the flight leader that members of the flight had been unable to locate the recommended landing strips on the salt flats. During a discussion of emergency procedures prior to the flight; Col. Norman had expressed his confidence in the F-86H to be suitable for a gear-up forced landing, thus disagreeing with the other pilots.

Unfortunately the extended speed brakes had a marked effect upon the glide distance of the F-86H. The condition added 1680 FPM rate of sink to the 1710 FPM rate normally encountered. An F-86H aircraft with a wind milling engine below 10,000 feet and 200 knots indicated airspeed, would have a total sink rate of 3390 FPM with the speed brakes extended.

With a clean aircraft, glide distance would have been 11.7 miles, 3.5 minutes glide at 200 knots indicated airspeed. It therefore appeared that the pilot had an even chance of making the runway if the speed brakes had been retracted. The reason for the extension of the speed brakes remained undetermined but possibly the switch had been put into neutral position rather than to the "full in" position. It was found by tests of the engine which survived relatively intact, that the primary cause of the accident was a malfunction within the fuel system.

F-86H, 52-2082: CRASH SITE TODAY

The crash site of F-86H, serial number 52-2082, is located approximately two miles north of the Wendover airport, Wendover, Utah. By using old grainy accident report photos, our seven member group set out searching for two F-86 Sabre crash sites in the same area with this one being relatively easy to find. Craig Fuller of Aviation Archaeology Investigation and Research had brought along photos that easily matched the terrain to the northwest of the Bonneville Salt Flats. We had decided to drive east and west until the photos aligned, then park our vehicles and walk a small grid. Before we could do that, Craig stopped his

Toyota Tacoma truck and pointed at the ground indicating that he had found aircraft debris next to his truck. We were all surprised that he had found this site so fast.

On first examining the site, we found that everything in view and what had been written in the accident report all corresponded with what we had read about this accident. The entire area was covered in several inches of salt and there were dirt mounds rising up with brush growing on their tops that dotted the landscape. Walking between the mounds we started finding small badly corroded parts of the F-86 scattered over a distance of approximately one-hundred yards. In several areas there were .50 caliber shell casings with unfired primers all within the same area as the wreckage. It was not determined if these came from the crashed plane or from something else, but one thing that was kind of suspicious though, was that the bullets were missing. This scenario we find often at other sites with the bullets normally being dislodged by kinetic energy in the event of hard impacts. Other items found included thick Plexiglas from the canopy, engine fittings, and airframe parts.

After documenting this site we started a search further to the east in search of the second F-86 Sabre. The new search area was incredibly scenic with salt flats and rock formations and after several hours of intense searching; we had turned up nothing. It was getting toward late afternoon so our group decided to enjoy a nice visit to the Bonneville Salt Flats. Latter on it was determined that we had been about one mile off course from finding the second F-86 crash site. The September weather couldn't have been better and we all had a great time.

The North American F-86H Sabre in this photo closely resembled the F-86H, serial number 52-2082, which crashed north of Wendover, Utah on 20 August 1955 killing Colonel Henry H. Norman. (U.S. Air Force)

Smoke rises from the crash of F-86H, serial number 52-2082, in this original accident report photo taken two miles north of Wendover AFB, Wendover, Utah. (U.S. Air Force)

Fire and rescue personnel inspect the wing from the crashed F-86H Sabre that claimed the life of Colonel Henry H. Norman. (U.S. Air Force)

The forward fuselage and wing can be seen in this accident report photo at the crash site of Col. Norman's North American F-86H, serial number 52-2082. (U.S. Air Force)

Vicki McCurry and Rasa Fuller take a break from exploring the F-86H crash site while Craig Fuller, Don Hinton, and Dave Trojan continue documenting the site in the background. (Photo by Dave McCurry)

Badly corroded airframe part and .50 caliber ammo casing at the F-86H crash site. (Photo by Dave McCurry)

The salt-covered ground quickly corrodes aluminum aircraft parts. (Photo by Dave McCurry)

The mountain range in the background made it fairly easy for Craig Fuller to find this F-86H site by matching original accident report photos. (Photo by Dave McCurry)

Several thick pieces of Plexiglas from the F-86's canopy were seen around the crash site. (Photo by Dave McCurry)

Parts from the crashed F-86H Sabre were found scattered over a one-hundred yard wide area. (Photo by Dave McCurry)

Dave McCurry examines some of the debris at the crash site of F-86H, serial number 52-2082, located near Wendover, Utah. (Photo by Vicki McCurry)

Chapter 13

High Altitude Stall Downs P-47D Thunderbolt

By David L. McCurry

LIEUTENANT Aikens V. Smith whom was a roommate with 2nd Lieutenant Theodore Norpoth visited with Lt. Norpoth on the flight line at about 6:30 PM, July 4, 1944 and then saw him later at the Officers Club at about 9:30 PM. Lt. Norpoth's parents had arrived the evening before and he had just returned from visiting with them. Lt. Smith didn't see Lt. Norpoth again until the following morning because he had attended a barbeque that night and then went to bed early. Although Lt. Smith didn't hear him come in, he speculated that Lt. Norpoth had come in very late. When Lt. Smith got up the next morning, he called Lt. Norpoth at about 6:50 AM reminding him that he had to be in ground school by 7:30 AM. At the time that he had awoke him, Lt. Norpoth seemed to be exceptionally sleepy and Lt. Smith had a hard time awakening him.

On July 5, 1944, Acting Crew Chief Pvt. Edwin J. Wilson on P-47D, serial number 42-28210, noticed while walking out to the Thunderbolt aircraft with Lt. Norpoth that he looked very tired. He remarked "Lieutenant, you look very tired" to which Lt. Norpoth answered, "yes, I am very tired." Not knowing that Lt. Norpoth had failed to report to the flight surgeon on July 5, 1944 for a pre-flight medical briefing prior to take-off; Pvt. Wilson helped Lt. Norpoth start the aircraft prior to Norpoth taxiing out for departure.

The weather on this day at Wendover Field, Utah was 6,000 feet broken with a surface visibility of 20 miles and winds NW at eighteen miles per hour. The U. S. Army Air Forces Accident Report stated that 2nd Lt. Theodore Norpoth flying the Republic P-47D, 42-28210, departed Wendover at 1645 (PWT) Pacific War Time on a high altitude acrobatic and individual combat mission. He was one of a flight of three assigned to the 2nd Air Force, 72nd Wing, 216th AAF base unit at Wendover and led by Captain Magnus W. Francis, an instructor pilot.

Captain Francis had scheduled Lt. Norpoth and Lt. Murphy for a high altitude acrobatic mission and told them that their mission was restricted to slow rolls, chandelles, and lazy eights because of the stalling characteristics of the P-47 at that altitude. He had also told them to check the oxygen equipment in their airplanes.

It took approximately thirty minutes to climb to an altitude of 23,000 feet and then Captain Francis pulled away and above them so the two pilots could start with slow rolls. Lt. Norpoth was the first to start with a slow roll and did one good slow roll to the left, then climbed back up to what appeared to be the original altitude that he had started at. After climbing back to altitude, Captain Francis observed Lt. Norpoth execute a diving turn to the right flying under him to a point where he could no longer see him. Captain Francis pulled away to watch Lt. Murphy do his acrobatics and then shortly afterward looked for Lt. Norpoth whom was nowhere to be seen. He tried to contact him by radio to advise him that he was running low on fuel and they would cancel the mission and return to the field. Captain Francis and Lt. Murphy looked for him all the way down to 6,000 feet indicated altitude but could not locate him. At this point they assumed that Lt. Norpoth had returned back to the field.

Captain Arthur B. Richie whom was returning to the field from a completed mission at about 1720 (PWT) was circling south of the field waiting for landing clearance when he noticed a puff of smoke to the southwest of the field. He then flew over to investigate and realized it to be a crashed plane. He reported the crashed plane to be burning in a ravine approximately 12 miles southwest of Wendover Field. After calling the crash in, Captain Richie was forced to return to the field because of a lack of fuel and then reported to Base Operations.

A search party reaching the crash scene identified the plane as being the one flown by Lt. Norpoth. It had exploded upon impact with the ground throwing debris and burning gasoline for a considerable distance killing Lt. Norpoth instantly. Lt. Norpoth had apparently not attempted to use his parachute since the safety belt although burned, was found in the fastened position. It was never determined whether this accident was caused by high altitude stalling or possibly hypoxia.

The remains of Lt. Norpoth's P-47 were so badly

destroyed that an investigation was not possible, and the accident was then considered undetermined.

P-47D Thunderbolt: Crash Site Today

Driving through several large washes to reach the crash site of P-47D, 42-28210, we were fortunate to have the use of Craig Fuller's 4WD Toyota Tacoma pickup truck to shuttle our aircraft wreck hunting group to and from the site. The site located southwest of Wendover, Utah is fairly remote. It took a while to figure out which desert ravine the crash site was located in, but with six of us searching, we were eventually able to find it. Bits of wreckage from the P-47D are spread out over a huge area indicating a very high speed impact. While visiting this site we were visited by two wild horses that were very curious of us.

At the main impact site located below a hill, we found mainly engine parts from the aircraft's 2,535 horse power Pratt & Whitney R-2800 Double Wasp radial engine. There were pieces of engine cylinders, engine valves, and valve springs all located in this area. Moving up a small rise, there was burned and badly mangled airframe parts of all kinds. Off to the side of the debris field our group located some side plates from one of the P-47's eight .50 caliber Browning machine-guns. Other items seen at the site were cockpit items which included a fuel indicator gauge and a pitch trim indicator gauge.

Formation of Republic P-47 Thunderbolts over Italy in April of 1944. (Photo U.S. Army Air Forces)

Remnants of 2nd Lieutenant Theodore Norpoth's Republic P-47D, which crashed on 5 July 1944, are scattered all over this landscape located twelve miles southwest of Wendover, Utah. (Photo by Dave Trojan)

Crumpled aluminum debris as seen in the foreground is scattered over a half-mile area after the high-speed crash of Lt. Norpoth's P-47D, serial number 42-28210. (Photo by Dave Trojan)

Vicki McCurry looks out over the desert landscape while proceeding on to the impact site of Lt. Norpoth's P-47D fighter plane. (Photo by Dave McCurry)

Access door from the P-47 wreck located half-way through the crash debris field. (Photo by Dave McCurry)

Overhead view of some of the P-47's crash debris. (Photo by Dave McCurry)

Inspection cover probably coming from one of the P-47's wings. (Photo by Dave McCurry)

To the left side of the crash path, we found these parts from a Browning .50 caliber machine-gun. (Photo by Dave McCurry)

Several cockpit items found at the crash site included this fuel gauge. (Photo by Dave McCurry)

Another cockpit item found at the site was this elevator trim indicator. (Photo by Dave McCurry)

While visiting the P-47D crash site, we were visited by two wild horses that were very curious of us. (Photo by Dave McCurry)

At the impact site of the P-47D, we noticed pieces of broken engine cylinders and valves from the aircraft's 2,535 horsepower Pratt & Whitney 18-cylinder radial engine. (Photo by Dave McCurry)

Chapter 14

Controlled Flight Into Terrain

By David L. McCurry

ON 12 February 1969, a General Dynamics F-111A, serial number 66-042, call sign FRUITY, was one of three aircraft scheduled to fly night low level navigation and bombing sorties within the Nellis Air Force Base local area. This aircraft was assigned to the 12th Air Force, 832nd Air Defense, 474th Fighter Wing, 4527th Combat Crew Training Squadron (CCTS), at Nellis AFB, Las Vegas, Nevada. The FRUITY aircrew was comprised of Captain Robert E. Jobe, Pilot, occupying the left seat, and Captain William D. Fuchlow, Instructor Pilot, occupying the right seat. Capt. Jobe and Capt. Fuchlow were assigned to the 4527 CCTS and Capt. Jobe was working towards upgrading to an instructor pilot status.

For their nighttime mission, F-111A 66-042 had a full internal load of fuel plus wing fuel for a total fuel load of 32,500 lbs. This aircraft was also configured with a SUU-20/A bomb/rocket dispenser containing 4 BDU-33 and 2 NX-106 practice bombs.

Two other F-111s, call signs RADIUM and TWIGGY, were scheduled to fly at the same time as FRUITY. Each aircraft was to fly individually with all aircraft performing the bombing portion of the mission during the same scheduled range period, 1720 PST to 1820 PST. Takeoff time for the three aircraft was scheduled for 1600 PST. The mission duration was to be three hours with the first portion being devoted to low level radar navigation training.

According to the United States Air Force Accident Report, Capt. Jobe and Capt. Fuchlow had planned to fly the Nellis low level route 15 to the Wendover Range for a dry bomb run on target number 7, then return to Nellis Bombing Range 3, a total distance of approximately 700 nautical miles.

The RADIUM Flight consisting of Major Robert D. McKelvey and Lieutenant Neil M. Pollock planned to fly Nellis low level route 9A before proceeding to Range 3 for bombing practice. The TWIGGY Flight consisting of Captain Henry R. Hutson and Captain Patrick V. Kennedy planned to fly Nellis low level route 13 before the bombing portion of the mission.

All three aircraft were scheduled on Nellis Range 3 at 1720 PST to deliver six bombs each. Sunset for this day was 1718 PST. The three crews briefed together and had preplanned to make entry times on the range with two minutes separation between aircraft. After completion of bombing, each crew had planned to accomplish a night auto Terrain Following Radar (TFR) letdown followed by night TFR training. The mission was briefed to terminate with an instrument approach and landing at Nellis AFB.

RADIUM took off from runway 21R at 1600 PST followed by FRUITY at 1602 PST and TWIGGY at 1605 PST. RADIUM made the standard North (visual) VFR departure to Dry Lake, which was 15 nautical miles north of Nellis AFB, and shortly afterward selected the auto TFR system and flew to the first turning point on their route. RADIUM reported the weather along this leg to be a broken ceiling, 10,000 to 14,000 feet above ground level (AGL) with visibility over 20 miles. Just prior to reaching their second turning point, RADIUM reported that the weather was getting progressively worse and a solid band of lower clouds was seen to the north of their course. When reaching the second turning point, which was located in a valley, RADIUM experienced a slight porpoise in the TFR system. They made a circle at that position to check out the TFR system and attributed the radar porpoise to the snow cover on the ground. These conditions can occur briefly over snow, water, and smooth terrain. At that point RADIUM terminated the low level route because of the deteriorating weather they could see to the north. RADIUM proceeded south toward Nellis and stated that the weather on their return route was the same as on the first leg of their flight.

TWIGGY navigated via route 13 to the third turning point at which time they terminated the low level route because of weather. TWIGGY reported that the weather obscured the mountains to the west of their course, and just to the north of turning point 3, the clouds extended to the floor of the valleys. TWIGGY turned to the southeast and proceeded back toward Nellis.

After takeoff at 1602 PST, FRUITY made a right turn out of traffic and shortly afterward, called Las Vegas Radar, and stated they were making a north departure. Las Vegas Radar acknowledged the call and informed FRUITY that they had radar contact. Godson Control, monitoring this frequency in accordance with standard procedures, called FRUITY and cleared them to range 3. FRUITY acknowledged this call, and approximately three minutes later, Las Vegas Radar informed FRUITY that radar service was terminated. FRUITY acknowledged the call and this was the last transmission heard from Capt. Jobe and Capt. Fuchlow. RADIUM and TWIGGY reported at the IP for Range 3 at 1719 and 1722 PST, respectively. They accomplished their bomb runs and departed the range at approximately 1800 PST. RADIUM and TWIGGY proceeded individually to the area north of Nellis, completed their mission, and then returned to Nellis for landing.

Nearly four months later, local rancher Irwin Griswold whom was riding horseback near the summit of the Pequop Mountains, was driving sheep ahead of him when all of a sudden the lead animals were spooked. Griswold rode ahead and saw what had frightened the animals. Flapping in the wind in one of the nearby trees was an orange and white parachute. As Griswold gazed across the terrain, he realized that he was looking at the crashed remains of the missing F-111.

The F-111A had impacted the snow covered southwest side of the Pequop Mountain Range just below the mountain's 9,249 foot summit scattering wreckage for over one and one-half miles distance. The crew of the FRUITY Flight, Captains' Jobe and Fuchlow, did not survive the accident.

The final determination into the cause of the F-111 accident by the investigation board pointed to the accident cause being Controlled Flight into Terrain (CFIT). Most F-111 variants included a terrain-following radar system connected to the autopilot and the accident was most likely caused by failure of the flight crew in noting the radar porpoise attributed to the snow cover on the ground, or possibly a malfunction of the autopilot.

F-111A, 66-042: Crash Site Today

The crash site of the General Dynamics F-111A is located 23 miles southeast of Wells, Nevada in the Pequop Mountain Range at an elevation of 9,100 feet above sea level. Jason Watt from Boise, Idaho and I had been discussing a visit to a nearby B-47E crash site in the Pequop mountains and decided to include a visit to both the F-111 and B-47 sites in one long day. After much discussion and many emails, we had invited a total of nine wreck hunting friends to meet in Wells on September 11, 2014, and visit the two sites during the following day.

Craig Fuller of Aviation Archaeology Investigation and Research had decided to volunteer the use of his Toyota Tacoma pickup truck to transport some of us up a crude seldom used mountain road to as high of an elevation on the mountain as possible. That left us a two mile hike and only a few hundred feet of elevation gain to the top of the mountain. Jason Watt used his Chevrolet van to transport the rest of us to a point as high as he could make it to before his van started bottoming out on large rocks. Unfortunately that punctured a hole in his oil pan. From there, Craig made a second trip traversing a high ridge line down in order to transport the rest of us to the top of the mountain.

After re-grouping, we conjured up a plan on how to hike to the F-111 site. With backpacks, ski poles, water, and plenty of food, we set off on what would become a very eventful day.

After an hour and a half of hiking we finally started sighting a few pieces of wreckage high on the mountain. The first large item that we had stumbled upon was one of the engines from the F-111 that had bounced over the west side of the ridge and part way down the east side. The engine was encased in mirror-like stainless steel and could be seen from quite a distance away. The next items we encountered as we climbed up the steep terrain were parts from the fuselage structure and radio circuit boards. As we crested the top of the mountain, we were all shocked to see that most of the wreckage from the F-111A swing-wing plane was still scattered across the mountain.

We hadn't planned for more than a few hours of time in documenting the F-111 site, but because of the amount of wreckage left at the crash site, we were overly intrigued with exploring the remains and wound up spending most of the day there. That really put a serious time limit on us making it to the B-47E site before darkness.

As we descended down the west side of the mountain, one thing that really stood out was the entire vertical stabilizer lying on the slope, intact with a nice bronze plaque attached to it. Also located nearby was the plane's rudder. Descending down a little further below the tree line, we could see a line of wreckage that extended for over a one mile distance. Looking at the initial impact point, it appeared as though the F-111 may have been in a shallow climb but still level with the angle of the terrain. There wasn't much of an imprint left in the ground and there were a lot of large pieces of the plane scattered in a straight line indicating a slow deceleration while breaking off large parts as it moved up the slope. Not realizing how late it had gotten, we re-grouped again and set off to find the B-47E.

Our group arrived at the B-47E site at near darkness and it was decided that we would have to come back the following spring to correctly document that site. Rasa Fuller, Dave Trojan, and Jason Watt hiked back to the vehicles in order to retrieve us below the B-47 site, and after descending the mountain, it was discovered that Jason's van had leaked the crankcase oil out of the punctured oil pan, and it had to be towed off the mountain by Rasa. That made for a very long windy cold night, but the rest of our group was finally brought off the mountain when Rasa and Dave showed up in Craig's Toyota.

The General Dynamics F-111 Aardvark was a supersonic variable sweep-wing interdictor and tactical attack aircraft that also filled the roles of strategic bomber and electronic-warfare. It was powered by two Pratt & Whitney TF-30-P-100 turbofan engines giving it a service ceiling of 66,000 feet and top speed of Mach 2.5. (U.S. Air Force)

Vicki McCurry stands on the 9,249 foot summit of the Pequop Mountains, 23 miles southeast of Wells, Nevada, in preparation for the hike to the F-111A, serial number 66042, crash site. The site is located two miles south of this location in the background. (Photo by Dave McCurry)

Some of the first items from the crashed F-111A that we came across. This debris along with an engine was located on the opposite ridge and more than a mile from the impact area. (Photo by Dave McCurry)

Dave McCurry arrives at an engine from the F-111 encased in brilliant shining stainless steel. (Photo by Vicki McCurry)

Looking down the mountain as others from our hiking group arrive at the F-111's engine. (Photo by Dave McCurry)

Seven of the nine members from our hiking group pose behind the rudder from the wrecked F-111 fighter-bomber. (Photo by Vicki McCurry)

A flag was placed at the F-111's vertical stabilizer in memory of Maj. Robert E. Jobe and Maj. William Fuchlow. (Photo by Dave McCurry)

Don Hinton holds his hand above a fragment from the F-111A aircraft which is still embedded in this tree. The right stabilator (upside down in this photo) and part of the rear fuselage where it came to rest after knocking down the tree in 1969. (Photo by Vicki McCurry)

Bronze memorial plaque attached to the vertical stabilizer from F-111A, serial number 66042. (Photo by Dave McCurry)

Right rear half of the crew escape module. Note the blue rubberized canvas of the flotation bag at right rear. This was used in case of the capsule landing in water. (Photo by Dave McCurry)

Placard reads Ejectable Crew Module. (Photo by Dave McCurry)

A pivot joint from one of the F-111's swing-wings. (Photo by Jason Watt)

Wreckage from the aircraft still shows its vivid colors. (Photo by Dave McCurry)

Looking downhill toward the F-111's impact site, you can see wreckage scattered all over the mountainside for more than one mile. (Photo by Dave McCurry)

Standing at the impact site, Jason Watt inspects a nose wheel door from the F-111A. (Photo by Dave McCurry)

Chapter 15

Failure of Engine Turbine Wheel Severs Aft Fuselage from F-86D Sabre

By David L. McCurry

1ST Lieutenant Finlay B. Wallace couldn't possibly have picked a better day for a test flight of the F-86D Sabre, serial number 52-10081. On this clear calm day of 12 December 1955; shortly after takeoff, engine problems suddenly created a tragic end to his flight.

The United States Air Force Accident Report stated that Lt. Wallace had taken off in the North American F-86D from Larson Air Force Base, Moses Lake, Washington, on a routine operational check in the local area following a replacement of the elevator trim actuator. Wallace performed a maximum performance takeoff and climbed to an estimated 20 to 25,000 feet of altitude. At approximately 0810 local time, eyewitnesses reported observing the aircraft on fire and hearing three explosions or unusual sounds in rapid succession as the aircraft broke apart and began falling to the ground. The aircraft assigned to the 538th Fighter Interceptor Squadron and based at Larson AFB had only been airborne for five minutes.

The aft section of the F-86D was torn from the fuselage by segments of the Timken alloy rim of the turbine wheel from the aircraft's General Electric J47-GE-33 turbojet engine, which severed the two lower fuselage attach point fittings. The wings were then torn away from the forward fuselage during the ensuing tumbling action with the fuselage coming to rest approximately two miles from the point where the tail section had broken away. Wreckage was scattered along a northwesterly flight path for approximately three and one-half miles.

Evidence showed that the canopy and seat charges had been fired after the break-up suggesting a successful ejection. However, Lt. Wallace's body and the ejection seat landed within a few feet of each other with evidence that the seat became entangled with the parachute canopy and right shroud lines. The ejection seat and Wallace's body were located approximately three quarters of a mile from the main fuselage impact point which indicated that that the ejection phase of the escape was performed at a considerable altitude. Insufficient time for a complete parachute deployment or the tangling of the chute canopy with the ejection seat prevented the completion of a successful bailout resulting in a fatal injury to Lt. Wallace upon contact with the ground.

Twenty-seven year old Lt. Wallace was married and in excellent health with no known physical defects. He was intelligent and was an excellent pilot exceedingly well oriented in military aviation with considerable experience in the F-86 aircraft. Lt. Wallace loved to fly and was considered by most members of his squadron as a superior pilot if not the best in the squadron. His experience level in this aircraft as well as other jet aircraft was far above average.

FINDINGS

The primary cause of the accident was material failure of the turbine wheel as evidenced by the recovery of segments of the Timken alloy rim which separated from the turbine wheel cone at the weld. The aft section of the empennage became separated from the forward fuselage due to disintegrating segments of the turbine wheel rim severing the two lower aft-fuselage section attach fittings. The wing spars were buckled by a severe positive load factor being applied on them by the forward fuselage pitching upward when the two lower fuselage attach fittings were severed. This was evidenced by the main gear locks being broken and both main wheels being extended and locked. The fuselage then pitched downward when the aft fuselage broke off resulting in severe negative loads being imposed on the wings causing them to tear from the fuselage.

The three explosions or unusual sounds reported by witnesses could have been coming out of the afterburner followed by the turbine wheel disintegration. Other possibilities could have been the aft section separating from the fuselage and both wings being torn from the fuselage accompanied by a fuel fire.

After releasing the canopy, Lt. Wallace ejected from the remains of the aircraft at an unknown altitude. He apparently then unfastened the lap belt and shoulder harnesses after losing his helmet and mask assembly, and probably then pulled the automatic release and D ring after being partially separated from the seat at an extremely low altitude. The ejection seat falling at a slightly slower rate was apparently above Lt. Wallace, and on the opening of the parachute, entangled in the right shroud lines preventing full deployment of the chute shortly before impact with the ground.

The canopy was found almost two miles from the fuselage lying upside down with the glass broken from impact. Deep gashes and streaks of white paint from Lt. Wallace's helmet were found on the inside of the canopy glass. Blood was also found on the inside of the canopy indicating that Lt. Wallace had been injured from tremendous stresses and turbulence before the canopy was ejected.

The fuselage landed almost flat on its left side on the southeast side of a small rocky natural crater. After impact, the fuselage had slid about fifteen feet coming to rest with the forward end just touching the bottom of the crater. It was badly burned from the rear of the cockpit area to the aft end. Soot found on the outside of the nose section indicated a flash fire had occurred before impact. The same evidence was found on the outside of the canopy frame and had occurred before the canopy release. This appeared to have been caused by burning fuel from the left wing fuel cell which was ruptured when the left wing was broken off. All twenty-four rockets on board, although badly broken, were found within twenty-five feet of the rocket pod area. Because of the severe damage incurred by the impact, it was impossible to determine the position of any switches but the throttle was almost half way to the Military Stop. All instrument glasses were broken and most of the pointers were missing. The basic engine from the accessory section to the turbine girdle aft flange was found in the remains of the main fuselage, while the afterburner and nozzle assembly was found in the aircraft's severed aft section. Turbine wheel rim segments were found scattered throughout a one mile area, approximately two miles from the main fuselage. Tragically, many good men have been lost in these situations where they had very little control.

F-86D, 52-10081: Crash Site Today

Very little remains today at the crash site of F-86D, serial number 52-10081, located four miles north of the small town of Marlin, Washington, but it is a unique site considering how the fuselage managed to fall into a small rocky natural crater located on private land. The crater itself has been virtually untouched while the surrounding area where the rest of the plane fell is flat and has been farmed over for the past sixty years.

Don Hinton of Spokane, Washington was led onto this crash site by Lauren Totusek who as a fifteen year old school boy witnessed the fuselage of the F-86D falling into the natural crater as he walked to school. Lauren vividly remembers walking through snow to the smoking remains of the fuselage and without an overwhelming interest, continuing on to tell his school buddies about it.

Our wreck hunting group met with Larry Lenz and his cousin, Lauren Totusek, who lives in Marlin, Washington, during October of 2014, to document this site as well as a Bell P-39Q Airacobra site located not too far from there. We crossed a well-manicured alfalfa field on foot to a rocky bowl shaped area that seemed far out of place. There didn't seem to be any logical reason for the natural crater to be there, so it appeared to us as a real oddity. The first things you spot after cresting the rim of the crater are several pieces of rocket launcher tubes lying out on the level floor of the crater. On closer inspection, we could then see that there were also airframe parts lying about. Of special interest, we noted there being pieces of the aircraft's instrument panel lying inside of the southeast side of the crater, and parts from the engine located on the outside of the northwest rim of the crater. That didn't make much sense to us so we are still trying to figure that one out.

The North American F-86D Sabre Jet (also known as a "Sabre Dog") was a transonic all-weather interceptor developed for the United States Air Force. It was powered by a General Electric J-47 turbojet engine and had a top speed of 693 mph. (Photo U.S. Air Force)

The severed aft fuselage section from North American F-86D, serial number 52-10081, lies in a snow covered field four miles north of Marlin, Washington, after an accident which claimed the life of Lt. Finlay B. Wallace on 12 December 1955. Note the afterburner and nozzle assembly from the J-47 engine still remaining inside of the aft section. (Photo U.S. Air Force)

The foreground in this photo is approximately where the ejection seat and pilot fell to earth. The fuselage from the F-86D fell to the left of the green area in the distance. (Photo by Don Hinton)

(From left to right) Don Hinton, Larry Lenz, and Lauren Totusek at the crash site of F-86D, 52-10081. As a fifteen year old school boy, Lauren witnessed the F-86D accident on his way to school, and was the first person to arrive at the smoking remains of the forward fuselage in the natural crater located north of Marlin, Washington. (Photo by Don Hinton)

Photo from the outer rim on the northwest side of the natural crater shows a close-up of stators from the compressor section of the F-86's J-47 engine. It was uncertain how part of the engine and fuselage impacted on the northwest outer rim of the crater area while the main portion of the forward fuselage impacted inside on the southeast edge of the crater. (Photo by Don Hinton)

Rocket launcher tubes were some of the first items found on the inside floor of the natural crater. (Photo by Don Hinton)

Photo taken from the south looking north inside of the natural crater shows Larry Lenz, Lauren Totusek, Vicki McCurry, and Don Hinton documenting parts of the crashed F-86D inside. Note the rocket launcher tubes lying on the ground in the bottom center of the photo. (Photo by Dave McCurry)

Pile of broken engine parts found on the northwest outer edge of the natural crater. (Photo by Don Hinton)

North American Aviation part number and stamp from the F-86D Sabre fighter jet. (Photo by Don Hinton)

Fin from the 2.75" FFAR (Folding Fin Aerial Rocket) found at the crash site of F-86D, serial number 52-10081. (Photo by Don Hinton)

Close-up of the imprinted info on the rocket fin, manufactured by ELKO in October of 1952. (Photo by Don Hinton)

This is the fuselage canopy sill from the F-86D with canopy rollers that engage the hooks on the canopy to latch it closed. (Photo by Don Hinton)

Dave McCurry inspecting some of the rocket tubes and other parts from the F-86D Sabre. (Photo by Don Hinton)

Two parts of clear Plexiglas with instrument data imprinted on them from the F-86D crash site. These are from the left and right secondary instrument panels that are to the left and right of the main instrument panel, angled 90-degrees from the panel. This was one of the most complex cockpits ever fielded, as the pilot had to do everything. They ran out of room to put instruments and switches so they added these two sub-panels. Also in the photo is a solid brass avionics box hand hold. (Photo by Don Hinton)

Chapter 16

Mid-Air Break-Up: The Touchet B-24 Tragedy

By David L. McCurry

WEATHER did not seem to be a factor as a formation of Consolidated B-24J Liberator bombers departed the Walla Walla Air Field, Washington, at 7:08 a.m. on July 19, 1944 on a high altitude formation and bombing training mission. Taking the lead was pilot 2nd Lieutenant John H. Spooner, and instructor pilot, Captain W. M. Harshbarger, flying B-24J AAF serial number 42-51617. The formation proceeded to the Boardman Bombing Range located in northeastern Oregon but was unable to bomb because of an unexpected overcast. The formation then began an ascent through the overcast and 51617 became separated from the group.

On their return trip to the Walla Walla Airfield, Lt. James W. Martin and his co-pilot, Lt. Nathan G. Richardson, flying B-24 number 579, at an altitude of 3500 feet, observed aircraft wreckage coming down out of the overcast. The wreckage was determined to be the fuselage and wings of a large aircraft along with hundreds of smaller parts falling along a path five miles long by two miles wide. After the wreckage had landed, the aircraft was then identified by the pilots as having been a B-24. The Walla Walla Tower was then notified of the accident by Lt. Martin just after 10:00 a.m. Lt. Martin continued circling the area until other planes came to the scene of the accident. From the air, Lieutenants Martin and Richardson could see people from farms located near the location of the crash investigating wreckage that had fallen throughout the area.

Just prior to the accident, a number of farmers working the fields approximately six miles north of Touchet, Washington, reported seeing the airplane spinning down out of the overcast then break up and crash. There were some conflicting reports from statements made by farmers living and working around the area, but most agreed with what they had witnessed.

Roy Dodd whom owned most of the property where the wreckage had fallen was driving his tractor and noticed bombers flying overhead at an altitude that they normally fly at. The next thing he noticed was bombs hitting the ground and starting fires. Seconds after seeing the bombs explode, Dodd looked up and noticed that one of the bombers was spinning and then observed a wing and tail flying off.

Investigation of the crash disclosed that all twelve members of the crew aboard 42-51617 were killed, and that there was no apparent attempt to jump. All personnel were wearing full high altitude clothing including oxygen masks. The aircraft had evidently broken up while in the overcast and at a very high altitude. There was no evidence of an explosion or fire other than small fires started from bombs landing in grassy areas. An indication of a high altitude break-up was noted by finding the heavier engines and nose section in one area followed by the lighter wreckage being found downwind over a path five miles long.

Those killed in the crash included: Capt. W. M. Harshbarger (instructor pilot); 2nd Lt. John H. Spooner (pilot); F/O Arthur L. Knowlton (co-pilot); F/O Kermit Peterson (navigator); K. E. McAllister (bombardier); W. R. Vigue (bombardier); Cpl. Leopold Wormuth; Cpl. William T. Pearl (radio operator); Pfc. John H. Worshan (gunner); Pfc. Ralph J. Winchester (gunner); Cpl. Robert N. Warren (gunner); and Pfc. Prince Thornton (gunner). All crewmembers were assigned to the Fourth Air Force, 423rd AAF Base Unit, Walla Walla, Washington.

INVESTIGATION CONCLUSIONS

The investigation board found the cause of the accident undetermined due to the complete destruction of the aircraft and the fact that the original break-up occurred at high altitude. Because of a lack of explosion or fire and the fact that it broke up at a high altitude, material failure was indicated, but conditions leading to such failure were undetermined. There were also no known mechanical deficiencies that might have been a contributing factor of the accident. The Instructor Pilot was probably at one set of controls as it was a formation flight, and he was considered to be an experienced competent pilot well able to handle any normal emergency. The accident investigation board had no recommendations.

TOUCHET B-24J: CRASH SITE TODAY

Six miles north of Touchet, Washington amongst

beautiful rolling hills of dry-land wheat, Don Hinton, along with my wife Vicki McCurry and myself, met with land owner Terry Schaeffer to tour the widely scattered crash site of B-24J, 42-51617. We had been communicating with Terry's neighbor, World War II Army veteran Delbert Dodd, whose mother Naomi had witnessed the B-24 accident while Delbert was fighting the war in Germany. Delbert whom has a 1957 crash site of a Stinson Voyager on his property referred us to Terry and that was how we got acquainted.

Delbert explained to us what his mother had told him about witnessing the accident. He remembered her telling him that she was standing outside watching the B-24s overhead when suddenly one of them started making a weird noise and then just exploded raining parts of the plane and bodies down over thousands of acres of their farm property. It was frightening and startled everyone around the adjoining properties. After being alerted, she noted that the army was quick in cordoning off the area and starting their investigation on what they thought was sabotage. Delbert's mother also told him that she was very surprised at how quickly the army removed the bulk of the wreckage as part of their investigation.

After a short meeting with Terry; he pointed out where two engines from the B-24 bomber had fallen high up on a plowed hill in view of his home. Then he drove us up a weedy dirt road on the north side of his property to an area where Terry's father had pointed out to him the site where the nose of the B-24 had impacted. Apparently the nose section, being partially buried, went unnoticed for a day or so before it was discovered by his father who had spotted a piece of metal sticking out of the ground. Terry hadn't actually seen any part of the plane in this area, but said that this was the area where the nose section had been located. Terry was nine months old when the accident happened so he didn't remember anything of it other than what he had been told.

Terry then drove us to a location about one mile south of this area to his family's old vacated home built during the latter 1800s and where Terry had grown up. It was fascinating to see this old home still in very good condition practically unchanged other than a small addition to the east side of the home. We followed another weedy dirt road from the house location, up the south side of his property to a location approximately one mile south of where the nose of the B-24 had been found. Here Terry pointed out an un-farmed hillside where he as a young kid remembered finding small pieces of wreckage that had fallen, and where part of the plane had also impacted. Terry, having other business to be contended with, drove us back to his farm home to board our own vehicle, then allowed us to tour the sites on our own.

Heading back to the north side where the nose section of the aircraft had impacted; we started metal detecting the area that Terry had pointed out to us. We immediately got a few hits and found some small one inch sized aluminum aircraft parts buried about twelve inches underground, but logically it seemed as though we should be finding something much more. As we moved uphill toward the dirt road, we started getting more hits and then started finding many larger parts. Apparently the nose section of the B-24 had impacted (if that is what it was then) the shoulder of the road. We found quite a few parts buried six to twelve inches below the surface that we readily identified as coming from the cockpit of the B-24 bomber. Some that were easily identifiable included nose framework, Plexiglas, a radio component box, and an oil temperature gauge.

After about three hours of documenting this site, we then drove to the other site one mile south of there. After no more than fifteen minutes of searching the hillside, we started finding a few heavier cast items probably coming from one of the B-24's engines. Over a one-half mile area we had found some small pieces of airframe and then Vicki found what appeared to be part of the bomber's engine cowling. While searching this area, she also found some pieces of Plexiglas. Don found some airframe parts and what appeared to be a heavier cast item from the tail turret which was buried in the plowed ground above the hillside. This may have been where the rear portion of the fuselage along with a wing and engine came down.

We made a second trip to the B-24 site two weeks later and combined it with searching for the civilian aircraft wreck on the property of Delbert Dodd. After searching a different area where wreckage from the B-24 had been reported by a farm worker; we found nothing more.

We had a nice meeting with Delbert and his wife where he shared with us his World War II experiences in Germany. Delbert now 91 years old, took part in the Battle of Remagen and others where he received three Purple Hearts because of injuries sustained from several ambushes by German soldiers. In two separate attacks, one being while he was riding on a half-track; Delbert was the lone survivor after the battles. He also spoke of nearly freezing to death during the Remagen operation.

The Battle of Remagen was a battle for control of the Ludendorff Railroad Bridge and the rapidly expanding Allied bridgehead on the eastern shore of the Rhine River. U.S. forces were able to capture and establish the first bridgehead across the Rhine River which was Germany's last major natural barrier and line of defense. To protect the bridge, the Americans positioned the largest concentration of antiaircraft weapons during World War II leading to the greatest antiaircraft artillery battles in American history.

Delbert's son, Delbert Jr., whom was visiting on the day of our visit, told us what he knew of the civilian aircraft wreck on their property stating that it happened about 1957, but never knew of what type of aircraft it was. Apparently this aircraft with two persons aboard was on the last leg of a trip home from Alaska when it encountered high winds at night, hit a plowed hill on the Dodd's property, and then crashed into a ravine fatally injuring its two occupants. Delbert Jr. explained that the aircraft was still in the ravine, and led us behind his pickup to the nearest point where we could then hike to the crash site.

After a short hike, we found the crash site without too much difficulty. Because of the condition of the wreck, it was hard at first to identify what type of aircraft it was. We soon realized that this was a fabric covered airplane and then discovered an aileron which appeared likely to have come from a Stinson aircraft. By looking at a wing strut and several other metal parts, everything started to fit in place as to what type of aircraft this was. I had wandered about 150 yards down the ravine and found what appeared only to be part of an exhaust system with a muffler attached. That was all that was showing, but after Don examined this part, he immediately determined that the entire engine was buried there probably by runoff. After removing some dirt from the underside of the engine, we rolled it over and discovered it to be an old six cylinder Franklin engine. After re-examining the rest of the wreck, it was fairly easy at this point to identify it as being a Stinson Voyager.

Formation of B-24s in the photo closely resembled the Consolidated B-24J, serial number 42-51617, piloted by Capt. W. M. Harshbarger, which crashed north of Touchet, Washington on July 19, 1944. (U. S. Army Air Forces photo)

The crash of Liberator 42-51617 occurred six miles north of Touchet, Washington over these beautiful rolling hills of dry-land wheat. (Photo by Dave McCurry)

Don Hinton and Vicki McCurry start a search in this area after being directed by Terry Schaeffer as to where the nose section of the stricken B-24 may have hit. Two very small aircraft parts were found in this area confirming that part of the plane did hit there. (Photo by Dave McCurry)

Near the shoulder of the dirt farm road we started getting more substantial hits on our metal detectors. This thick piece of Plexiglas from the nose turret area did confirm that the nose of the B-24 did impact there. (Photo by Dave McCurry)

Author Dave McCurry finds an oil temperature gauge from the B-24 wreck buried six inches below the surface. (Photo by Vicki McCurry)

After receiving several substantial metal detector hits; Don Hinton and Vicki McCurry start finding cockpit parts from the B-24 buried as deep as twelve inches below the surface. (Photo by Dave McCurry)

After nearly two hours of metal detecting the area, we were able to identify all of the items in the photo as having come from the nose and cockpit of the B-24. (Photo by Dave McCurry)

On our way to another impact area located about one mile away from the nose impact area, we stopped by Terry Schaeffer's old family farm house (now vacant) that was built in the late 1800s. (Photo by Dave McCurry)

On this hillside we started finding cast aluminum and small airframe parts from the B-24 that had fallen there. (Photo by Dave McCurry)

In this plowed field, Don Hinton found several aluminum internal parts from the B-24 that were buried about eight inches underground. (Photo by Dave McCurry)

Near the same area, Vicki McCurry spotted this heavy built aluminum piece that appeared to be part of an engine cowling with fasteners. She also found several pieces of Plexiglas nearby. (Photo by Dave McCurry)

This cast item found by Don Hinton appears to be part of the rear gun turret. (Photo by Dave McCurry)

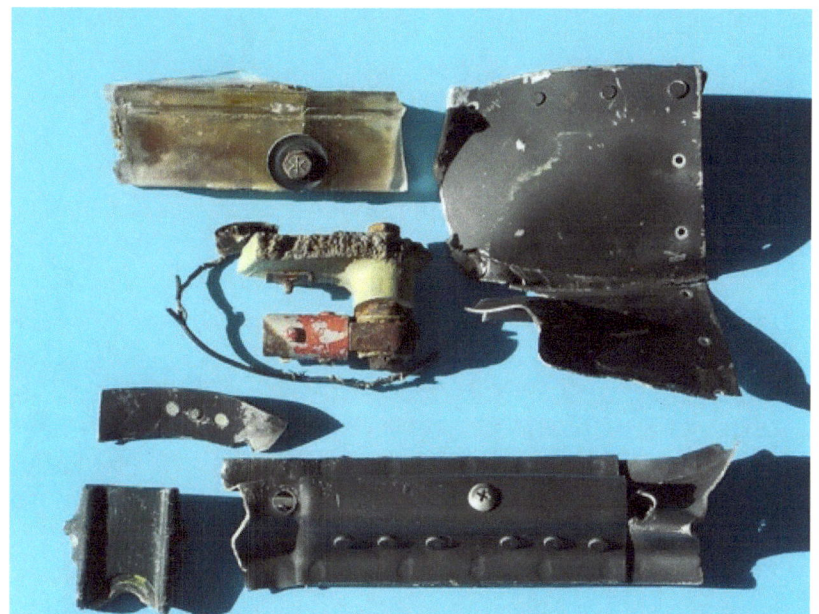

It was amazing to find these items in such incredibly good condition after being buried for more than seventy years. Items included thick Plexiglas, part of a radio tray, and aluminum framework from around the inside of the Plexiglas nose of the B-24. (Photo by Dave McCurry)

Close-up view of the oil temperature gauge from the B-24 bomber. (Photo by Don Hinton)

Chapter 17

Broken Connecting Rod Ends Airacobra Night Flight

By David L. McCurry

WITH a perfectly clear sky and unlimited visibility, 2nd Lieutenant Mark L. Lasly took off on a night cross-country flight departing from Moses Lake Army Air Field toward Spokane, Washington at 00:50 hours local time. He had been scheduled on this night of 18 July 1944 for a night navigation mission with takeoff time set at 00:51. After climbing to 7,000 feet of altitude, he started trimming the Bell P-39Q Airacobra, serial number 44-2328, for level flight, when the engine's manifold pressure started to drop. He increased the throttle setting slightly and the engine exploded. Without any hesitation, Lt. Lasly immediately bailed out of the aircraft at 7,000 feet northwest of Odessa, Washington. At the time of his successful bail-out; Lasly noted the time as being 01:10. The aircraft fell off into a slow descending turn before impacting the ground where it exploded and burned after crashing. The P-39Q had been based at Moses Lake, Washington, and assigned with the 4th Air Force, 431st Base Unit.

ACCIDENT CAUSE

According to the U. S. Army Air Forces Accident Report, an examination of the crash site of 44-2328 disclosed that the Allison V-1710-85 engine had hit with such force that it was broken into several pieces. It was discovered that the crankshaft journals in the vicinity of the number six cylinder were burned and distorted. The connecting rod of the number six cylinder was also found to be burned and broken at the fork.

The investigation board was of the opinion that there was a loss of oil due to a leak of undetermined origin causing a connecting rod failure. The explosion referred to was probably a connecting rod breaking, and going through the engine crank case. During the preceding three days prior to this accident, oil leaks had been noted and repaired by maintenance personnel. Citing a difference of opinions, a definite responsibility could not be established, but indications were pointing toward a possibility of improper maintenance.

P-39Q, 44-2328: CRASH SITE TODAY

Through the help of Lauren Totusek of Marlin, Washington, along with his cousin Larry Lenz, we were able to locate the crash site of P-39Q, 44-2328, on the edge of a canyon four miles northwest of Odessa, Washington. Before visiting the site, Lauren being a native of the area, shared a lot of stories with us in regard to World War Two U.S. Army Air Corps. flight training that he had witnessed in the area as he was growing up. Some of the stories included having four-engine bombers and fighter planes flying over their tractors so low that they dove off onto the ground thinking the planes might hit the tractor's vertical exhaust pipes. On our way to visit the P-39 crash site, we first visited his family's old homestead from the 1920s. We stopped at a point along the road where Lauren pointed out to where an old windmill used to stand. This apparently was where Lieutenant Lasly landed by parachute at night, and with him nearly getting hung up on the windmill. This was also the area where Lauren had found a door from the P-39Q out in his wheat stubble field that he had kept propped against his old barn for many years.

The next stop was a visit to an old farm house that Lauren had lived in as a kid which was more than one-hundred years old. Lt. Lasly had stayed with Lauren's family in this house until he was picked up by the army. It was amazing for us to see a property and all of its contents that had virtually stood unchanged for most of those years. Outside of the home we saw an old wagon and rusted farm machinery that dated back into the latter 1800s. The machines had been parked for so long that they were slowly settling into the ground. An interesting item that Lauren had to show us in the barn was an original 1947 Dodge truck that his family had bought new. The truck was still in running condition and had its original paint and upholstery.

Our group which included Don Hinton, Dave and Vicki McCurry, along with Larry and Lauren, loaded our backpacks and cameras into Lauren's four-wheel-drive Ford pickup and headed down a steep dirt road into a canyon not far from the old homestead.

We parked on the edge of an old dry lake bed where Lauren pointed to an area that the crash site was located in. Lauren hadn't been to the crash site for more than thirty years and was a little confused as to exactly where it was located. He remembered it being on the edge of the lake bed in which we searched for a while and found nothing. We then decided to split up and search areas along the canyon within one mile of where Lauren remembered seeing debris from the P-39. After nearly two hours of searching along and on top of the canyon, our group was nearly ready to give up the search. Never willing to easily give up, I had one more idea? I would hike half way up the canyon in the opposite direction for no more than one mile, then turn back. As I started along, I was surprised to find an aircraft part sitting alone part way up the canyon and within about fifteen minutes of hiking. I immediately knew then that I was about to stumble upon the crash site. With the excitement of finding the part, I started hollering at Don who was way off in the distance. None of the others could hear me, but Don finally caught on that I had found the site. He alerted the others and the rest of the party started a slow ascent up to where I was.

I had found a few more parts of the P-39 by the time everyone else arrived. On the way up, Vicki found the impact crater which was located about one-hundred yards north of my position. The first thing we all noticed was that the impact site overlooked a vertical cliff above the floor of the dry lake bed. Lauren remarked that what he had seen years before was debris on the lake bed. He never knew that the impact site existed up along the canyon wall. Apparently what he had found years ago was parts from the P-39's Allison engine and other debris that had ricocheted off the cliff and onto the lake bed. We were all a little surprised about that.

On investigating the impact crater we noticed lots of engine parts that included engine cylinder liners, small accessories, broken cast aluminum crankcase parts, and bent exhaust pipes. There were also a number of .50 caliber brass machine-gun casings imbedded into the crater. Outside of the impact area there was airframe parts scattered in all directions. Rocks were located in front of the impact site and it appeared as though many of the parts had bounced off the rocks scattering them to the sides of the crash path. Time restraints didn't allow us to study the site as well as what we would have liked, but nevertheless, it was a very interesting trip.

Bell Aircraft P-39 Airacobra in this 1944 Solomon Islands photo closely resembled 2nd Lieutenant Mark Lasly's Airacobra that crashed northwest of Odessa, Washington on the night of 18 July, 1944. (U.S. Army Air Corps.)

Wreckage from Lt. Lasly's P-39Q seen in the foreground while overlooking the dry lake bed near Odessa, Washington. (Photo by Dave McCurry)

Original accident report photo of the crash site of of P-39Q, serial number 44-2328. (U.S. Army Air Corps.)

First part found by author Dave McCurry signaled the eventual location of the crash site of P-39Q, 44-2328. (Photo by Dave McCurry)

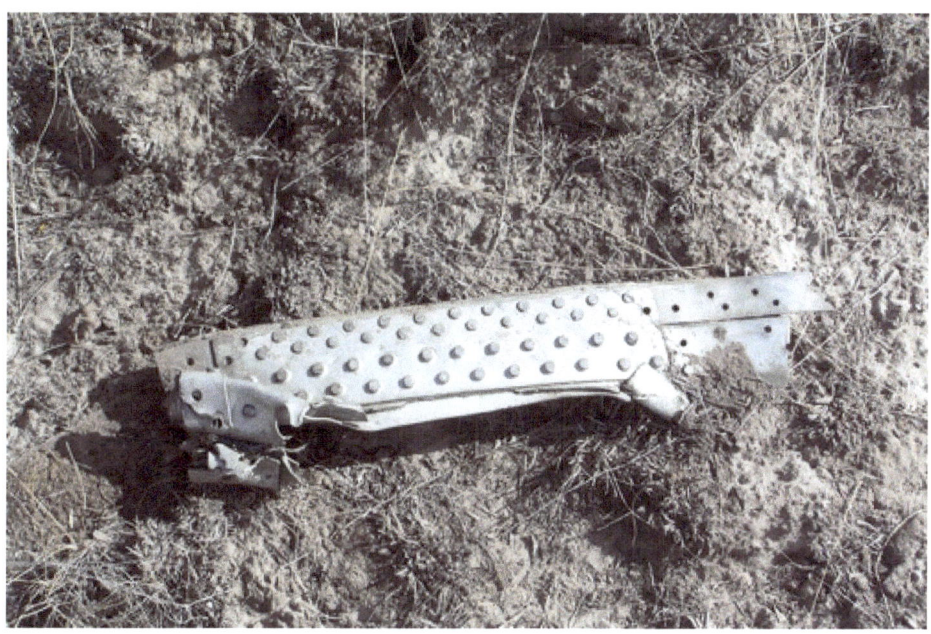

Other parts like this one led us to the impact crater left after the 1944 Airacobra crash. (Photo by Dave McCurry)

Vicki McCurry pictured on the left found the P-39's impact crater. Also pictured are Lauren Totusek (center) and Larry Lenz (far right). (Photo by Dave McCurry)

Close-up view of one of the larger pieces of wreckage that we found at the site. (Photo by Dave McCurry)

This piece of wreckage from the P-39Q still shows some of its olive-drab paint. (Photo by Dave McCurry)

From left to right: Larry Lenz; Lauren Totusek; Don Hinton; and Vicki McCurry; as they document the impact crater of P-39Q, 44-2328. Note the rock formation in the background that matches the original accident report photo. (Photo by Dave McCurry)

Several large pieces of Plexiglas were noted at the site. (Photo by Dave McCurry)

Very interesting rock formations encompass the P-39's crash site in this region of Washington, State. (Photo by Dave McCurry)

Dave McCurry examines one of the Airacobra's exhaust stacks at the crash site of P-39Q, 44-2328. (Photo by Vicki McCurry)

Door from P-39Q, 44-2328, which was found by Lauren Totusek in his wheat stubble field. This unique find sat leaning against his barn for many years. (Photo by Dave McCurry)

Inner view of the door from the P-39Q. Note the aircraft's serial number, 44-2328, in yellow paint stencil on the bottom of the door. (Photo by Dave McCurry)

Chapter 18

The Salish Peak F-89s

By David L. McCurry

WITH a cloud ceiling estimated at 2,000 feet above sea level and layers up to 30,000 feet in intermittent light rains, a practice scramble and subsequent training mission was scheduled for two Northrop F-89D Scorpion fighter planes operating out of Paine Air Force Base, Washington, on March 2, 1956. The two aircraft flown by 1st. Lieutenants Willford Hall Taylor and Hal Nathan Williams were assigned to the 25th Air Division, 326th Fighter Group, 321st Fighter Intercept Squadron, and based at Paine Field AFB. Also aboard were Lt. Taylor's Radar Operator, Phillip E. Gereau and Lt. William's Radar Operator, William E. Von Driska.

At approximately 1050 PWT "Household Control," a radar facility located in Blaine, Washington, complied and scrambled Sixpence Charlie One and Two as a flight with three hours of fuel and Paine AFB being both the departure point and destination. "Charlie One" serial number 53-2647A was airborne at 1056 PWT, and "Charlie Two" serial number 53-2641A was airborne at 1100 PWT. They made an Instrument Flight Rules (IFR) climb, breaking out on top of the overcast at 37,000 feet of altitude. Household set the two aircraft up for a practice intercept, using Charlie One as the target and Charlie Two as the interceptor.

Shortly after the final intercept vector was given to Charlie Two, Household lost radio contact with Charlie Two. Household maintained contact with Charlie One and Charlie One reported he had loud and clear contact with Charlie Two. From this time on, Household took no further aggressive control action.

Household monitored Charlie One and Charlie Two's radar join-up, with Charlie One in the lead position three to five miles ahead. Household Control had difficulty maintaining radio contact with Charlie One as he was apparently changing channels attempting to improve contact with Charlie Two.

Charlie One requested weather at Paine, McChord, and Larson Air Force Bases and was told that if he waited a short time, the latest weather would be available. Charlie One then replied that he would wait. At this time Charlie One also reported loud and clear radio contact with Charlie Two.

The Following weather was transmitted to Charlie One: Clouds 1600 scattered 2500 overcast, seven miles visibility with light rain, altimeter setting 29.96. Charlie One then repeated the altimeter setting as being 996. McChord was forecast 2000 scattered, measured 3000 overcast, six miles visibility, with light rain. Larson was 14,000 scattered, 18,000 thin overcast, and 15 plus miles visibility. Charlie One acknowledged all weather.

Charlie One requested a letdown at Paine with 1145 PWT being the approach time. He requested an Automatic Direction Finder (ADF), Ground-Controlled Approach (GCA), with a 247 degree transition letdown from 37,000 feet to normal penetration altitude and stated it would be a lock-on approach for Charlie Two. Air Route Traffic Control (ARTC) approved the clearance as requested and added to enter the control area at 18,000 feet. Charlie One then acknowledged the clearance. Charlie One was instructed to give GCA a radio check on channel 16 and approximately one minute later, Charlie One reported loud and clear contact with GCA. This is a ground radar guided approach service provided by air-traffic controllers where they guide aircraft to a safe landing in adverse weather conditions, based on primary radar images. GCA claimed there was no contact made with them from Charlie One. The GCA team chief stated that he heard only the comment made on channel 16, "Can you stay on my wing?" This comment was not identified by a call sign.

At 1141 PWT Charlie One and Charlie Two radar paints merged on the Household radar scope and shortly after that, Charlie One instructed Household to delay his clearance by fifteen minutes. ARTC approved the delay and Charlie One was informed that his approach time would now be 1200PWT.

At 1143 PWT Charlie One reported VFR at 20,000 feet and requested an emergency straight-in approach to Paine. Household informed him that he was over mountains and he replied back that he was aware of this. ARTC then approved an ADF approach to Paine. Household did not receive the entire clearance and informed Charlie One that his emergency letdown had been approved and that he was cleared to start his decent.

Charlie One requested that Household inform him of his range from the Paine Homer marker beacon each five miles. Household acknowledged and informed his range was now 49 miles. At the 42 mile point, Charlie One was then asked the nature of his emergency. Charlie One stated, "left side fuel system not feeding." Charlie One was then informed that he was now 38 miles out.

At 1147 PWT Household advised Charlie One that he was still over mountains which Charlie One then acknowledged. Charlie One was then informed that he was now 35 miles out. Household requested Charlie One's altitude and Charlie One reported at 14,000 feet. Household then advised Charlie One not to descend below 7,000 feet before reaching Paine Homer. Less than one minute later after reporting at 14,000 feet, radar and radio contact was lost.

Various persons in and around Darrington, Washington, reported hearing jet aircraft flying unusually low, then the sounds of two subsequent explosions were also heard approximately five miles southwest of town. The two F-89s had crashed at 5,000 feet of elevation on Whitehorse Mountain southwest of Darrington killing all four airmen aboard instantly.

Following the crash, seven members of a mountain rescue group along with Major Kirk of Paine AFB, and Jim Battson, an aircraft manufactures representative, climbed to the crash sites of the two USAF jets on Whitehorse Mountain. The purpose of the trip was to make positive identification of the four missing airmen and to scout the area to determine the feasibility of evacuation of the remains. Members of the mountain rescue group included the leader, Max Eckenburg, famous mountain climbers Jim and Louis Whittaker, Dave Willis, Paul Williams, Arnie Campbell, and Rudy Miller. They reached the crash scene over a very rugged steep route and it was hoped that a helicopter could be used for the final recovery. Part of their operation was also to locate a suitable landing site.

SALISH PEAK CRASH SITES TODAY

Today the crash sites of both F-89D aircraft, serial numbers 53-2647A and 53-2641A, are located southwest of Darrington, Washington, on a ridgeline called Salish Peak between Whitehorse Mountain and Three Fingers Mountain. Both aircraft disintegrated on impact scattering small pieces of wreckage through talus and rock slabs just below the ridgeline. Part of the wreckage came to rest on a plateau at about the 5,000 foot level on the mountain. Out of the larger identifiable pieces; one item that really sticks out is the still highly visible Green Dragon insignia painted on the vertical stabilizer from the 321st Fighter Interceptor Squadron. Other visible large parts include large engine parts, wing and flap panels, and landing gears.

The Northrop F-89 Scorpion was the Air Defense Command's first fighter-interceptor to carry nuclear armament using air-to-air rockets equipped with nuclear warheads. Powered by two Allison J35 engines producing 7,200 pounds of thrust each with afterburner; the F-89 had a cruising speed of 465 mph and a maximum speed of 635 mph. (U.S. Air Force photo)

Wing panel with star from Salish Peak F-89 crash sites sits among piles of debris left over from the crashes of two F-89Ds, serial numbers 53-2647A and 2641A, which occurred on March 2, 1956. (Photo by Dave Fish)

Another star from the wing of one of the two F-89s that crashed on Salish Peak southwest of Darrington, Washington. (Photo by Brad Metz)

The painted-on Green Dragon insignia from the 321st Fighter Interceptor Squadron based at Paine AFB, Washington, is still highly visible on this vertical stabilizer from one of the crashed F-89 Scorpion fighter planes. (Photo by Brad Metz)

Overview of one of the F-89 crash sites shows part of the tail section sitting among scattered debris. (Photo by Brad Metz)

In this view you can see an engine and a flattened oxygen bottle in the background left over from one of the crashed Salish Peak F-89s. (Photo by Art Jackson)

Both aircraft as seen in this photo were completely disintegrated after crashing into Whitehorse Mountain. (Photo by Art Jackson)

One of the flaps from a crashed F-89 on Salish Peak. (Photo by Art Jackson)

Nose gear from one of the F-89s sits in a pile of talus. (Photo by Art Jackson)

Data plate from one of the two F-89's turbo-jet engines. (Photo by Art Jackson)

Radio receiver tuning panel from F-89 crash site. (Photo by Art Jackson)

Part of a rudder can be seen on the remains of this vertical stabilizer from one of the two Salish Peak F-89D Scorpion fighter aircraft. (Photo by Art Jackson)

Chapter 19

Ejection From F-86 Sabre Jet Conforms With Fire Warning Light

By David L. McCurry

AFTER making a walk around inspection on his North American F-86D, serial number 51-6020, Second Lieutenant Donn A. Byrnes climbed into the aircraft for his departure from Larson Air Force Base, Moses Lake, Washington. This aircraft attached to the 323rd Fighter-Interceptor Squadron at Larson was assigned to Lt. Byrnes on 2 October 1953, for a routine training mission.

The pressurization was set at 5 PSI and the trim was set for takeoff. All other checks were made in the cockpit and everything was indicating normal. After a normal start was made, the alternate, normal, and utility systems were checked and operating normally. The canopy was closed and locked before leaving the ramp for a run-up. The run-up to check the emergency system was completed and the RPM on the emergency system dropped to 94 percent and then stabilized. Lt. Byrnes then returned to the normal system and the RPM built back slowly to 100 percent. The tailpipe temperature was not noted while operating on the emergency system, but was 705 centigrade when the takeoff roll began at 0912 hours local time. Due to the fact that this was his second flight in an F-86D; Captain Paris D. Park was assigned to fly chase plane for Lt. Byrnes.

A normal takeoff was accomplished and at about 5,000 feet of altitude, the fuel system was switched to normal. As power was reduced from Military to 100 percent and 650 degrees centigrade tail pipe temperature, a slight surging and a tail pipe temperature fluctuation of about 25 degrees centigrade was noted. When power was reduced to 99 percent, the engine returned to a normal smooth operation.

After a climbing turn of about 140 degrees to the north, Lt. Byrnes reduced power further to 98 percent and 600 degrees centigrade tailpipe temperature. The Sabre Jet was climbing at 300 knots airspeed with a climb rate of 2100 feet per minute.

At approximately 15,000 feet, after being airborne for ten minutes, a turn to the right was initiated and at that time, the forward fire warning light began to flash. Lt. Byrnes immediately stop-cocked the engine in accordance with his pilot's operating instruction manual for the F-86D and informed Capt. Park of his difficulties. After stop-cocking the engine, the fire warning light went out. A check was made of the fire warning circuit and the indication was normal. Shortly after this time, the fire warning light came on and stayed on. There was no indication of any other trouble except for the warning light. Lt. Byrnes neither smelled nor saw smoke in the cockpit nor did he notice smoke emitting elsewhere from the aircraft. His oxygen regulator was set to the normal position. Capt. Park flying as chase pilot, was informed by Lt. Byrnes that the fire warning light was back on, and Capt. Park advised Lt. Byrnes to bail out after smoke was observed trailing from Lt. Byrne's aircraft. Lt. Byrnes then immediately ejected from the aircraft at 14,000 feet of altitude and at an indicated airspeed of 225 knots.

In preparation for ejection, Lt. Byrnes put both feet in the stirrups with his head back, and pulled both arm rests at the same time. The canopy departed and the cockpit was filled with fog. As soon as Lt. Byrnes was aware that the canopy was gone, he pulled the ejection trigger. As the charge went off, his head was thrust forward from the forces applied during the ejection. After the ejection, Lt. Byrnes remained physically conscious, but was unable to see the seat as he somersaulted violently three or four times. Finally Lt. Byrnes was able to release the harness belt. While tumbling with his chin strap unhooked, the force of the wind then pulled his helmet off.

As the safety harness was released, the chain pulled away but hung up on his right foot. Lt. Byrnes kicked it away and then pulled the rip cord as soon as he could reach it. He had the oxygen hose hooked to the right shoulder harness and believed that is what he had his foot caught on.

After the parachute opened, he looked up and saw that one panel had been ripped along the seam. Lt. Byrnes then made a very soft landing in a field of wheat stubble. It wasn't long before a farmer working in the area picked Lt. Byrnes up and took him to the town of Wilson Creek, where he then telephoned the base.

After Capt. Park made sure of Lt. Byrnes successful ejection and parachute opening, he followed the F-

86D and saw dark smoke streaming out with intermittent puffs coming from the tailpipe. He also noted smoke coming out from around the battery access door area on both sides. Capt. Park followed the aircraft down from 10,000 feet of altitude to where it crashed and exploded about ten miles northeast of Soap Lake, Washington. Then Capt. Park proceeded back to where Lt. Byrnes had landed and circled watching Lt. Byrnes wave to him indicating that he was okay.

ACCIDENT CONCLUSIONS

On arrival to the crash site of F-86D, 51-6020, investigators noted that the aircraft had impacted the ground at a five degree nose low angle scattering wreckage over a 900 yard long swath. Wreckage studied at the impact site showed no signs of an onboard fire prior to impact indicating the probability of a short circuit in the fire warning system.

The most probable cause of the accident was considered to be erroneous fire warning indications as a result of a forward fire warning system malfunction. The forward fire warning system installed in F-86D aircraft was vulnerable to abuse, deterioration, and insecurity.

The pilot's abandonment of the aircraft was in conformity with instructions contained in AN 01-60JLC-1, F-86D Flight Handbook of Instructions for Pilots, when the forward fire warning light illuminates during flight.

It was recommended that the forward fire warning system be redesigned to eliminate the inherent design inadequacies and the vulnerability of the system to damage during aircraft maintenance.

F-86D, 51-6020: CRASH SITE TODAY

What used to be an active Army Air Corps. and Air Force training area north of Soap Lake, Washington, is now rolling hills of dry-land wheat farms. There is no visible evidence today other than an occasional spent .50 caliber shell casing to tell the story of the huge aircraft training events that took place there. There are some existing aircraft crash sites located around the area, but it takes months if not years to find them. One in particular is the F-86D, serial number 51-6020, that crashed north of Soap Lake on 2 October 1953.

Constant plowing and erosion has changed the contour of the land to a point where it is difficult to match any of the original accident photos taken by the Air Force. While hiking around the general location of the crash site, we did accidently find part of the F-86D that crashed there, but today, there doesn't seem to be any logical way of finding the actual impact area. The part that we did find looked like one that someone had found while plowing a nearby field, then picked up and tossed along a fence line.

Surprisingly though, we did find a riveted aluminum part from an obvious P-39 crash site in the area that someone had tossed into a 1940s dump site. The area is very scenic especially during the spring wild flower season so we really enjoy hiking in the area whether we find any of the old wrecks or not.

The North American F-86D Fighter Interceptor was armed with 24 2.75 in. Mighty Mouse FFAR (Folding-Fin Aerial Rocket) rockets in a ventral tray. Photo is of early production USAF F-86Ds in formation. (Photo U.S. Air Force)

Tail section and forward fuselage of the F-86D Sabre Fighter Interceptor, serial number 51-6020, as it sits on the edge of plowed farm field ten miles north of Soap Lake, Washington. This aircraft piloted by Lt. Donn A. Byrnes crashed on 2 October 1953. (Photo U.S. Air Force)

Dave McCurry holding part of the F-86D's wreckage which was found within the general area of the crash site. Continuous plowing of the fields has changed the contour of the land making it difficult to identify the exact impact location. (Photo by Don Hinton)

North American part number identifies this as being an F-86D Sabre. (Photo by Dave McCurry)

This piece of wreckage from the F-86D was found near a fence post at the end of a fence line. There was no way of telling how it wound up there. (Photo by Dave McCurry)

North American Aviation stamp on the end of this piece of F-86 wreckage. (Photo by Dave McCurry)

Flip-side view of the small piece of F-86D wreckage. (Photo by Dave McCurry)

Chapter 20

Echelon Formation Creates Airacobra Collision

By David L. McCurry

WHILE flying straight and level at 10,000 feet in a loose formation of four P-39 fighter planes, flight leader, 2nd Lieutenant Henry Chew, gave the signal for an echelon formation to the right. Lt. Everett H. Wieslander was the element leader of the flight and was on the left side of the flight leader when he received the right echelon signal from his wing man, F/O Austin E. Welt. Wieslander had almost crossed all the way over from left to right when his plane gained altitude slightly, and Lt. Walter M. Turk, wing man to the flight leader, fell back a little. This movement caused their planes to crash together, Lt. Turk on top, and Lt. Wieslander on the bottom.

The mid-air accident involving Lt. Wieslander's Bell P-39K, serial number 42-4394, and Lt. Turk's P-39F, serial number 41-7235, occurred on May 27, 1944 northwest of the Ephrata AAF Base, Washington. On seeing that the two planes were going to collide, both Lt. Chew and F/O Welt peeled away with neither pilot observing the actual collision. Without witnessing the collision, it was impossible to determine where the two planes had hit each other.

After completing his turn Lt. Chew saw both planes spinning down and called to them continuously on the radio to bail out. Lt. Turk pulled out at between 4,000 and 5,000 feet and Lt. Wieslander never did recover from the spin. Five minutes before the accident, Lt. Chew had given a radio check and all radios seemed to be working fine.

Lt. Wieslander evidently was injured or his radio did not work after the collision because he stayed with the plane as it fell off into a flat spin. Lt. Chew repeated the "bail out" order nine or ten times but Lt. Wieslander either could not or would not comply with the order. According to one witness, the engine sounded like it was being gunned. This would indicate that Lt. Wieslander was injured and could not get out, or that the engine was running that way because of damage incurred in the collision. Lt. Wieslander's plane crashed and burned killing him instantly.

After recovering from the spin, Lt. Turk apparently under control, slowly spiraled down. Lt. Turk then attempted a wheels-up belly landing in a plowed field where the plane hit on its belly, bounced off the field, and continued on for another 200 feet. The plane came in fast and after the bounce either damaged some of its controls or Lt. Turk allowed the nose to drop too much. Lt. Turk's plane then hit hard nose first destroying the front half of his plane killing him as well.

Both planes were part of the Fourth Air Force, 430th AAFBU, Flight Section "D," based in Ephrata, Washington.

P-39K, 42-4394: Crash Site Today

Don Hinton along with my wife Vicki and I had been searching for the crash site of Lt. Wieslander's P-39 Airacobra for three years and we were finally led onto it by Todd Busby, the owner of a Seattle based hunting club. Because of reports from others, we had been searching an area two miles south of where we finally located the crash site, which is nine miles northwest of Soap Lake, Washington.

We were somewhat surprised to find quite a bit of debris still remaining at the site, but it is somewhat remote probably making it difficult to have removed all of the wreckage years ago. The Airacobra had impacted very hard on rocky ground scattering wreckage over a swath nearly 500 feet long.

At the impact site we noted quite a few 37mm cannon parts along with pieces of the Allison V-1710, 12 cylinder engine. Scattered throughout the rest of the site we found numerous .50 caliber ammo casings along with lots of airframe parts. One notable item that couldn't be missed was a rudder pedal and linkage located within the first third of the crash path.

The Bell P-39 Airacobra shown in this photo was very similar to the P-39K flown by Lt. Everett H. Wieslander which crashed northwest of Soap Lake, Washington, on May 27, 1944 following a mid-air collision. (U.S. Army Air Forces photo)

Original crash site photo of Lt. Wieslander's P-39K Airacobra, serial number 42-4394, taken shortly after the mid-air collision, shows the fire crew and ambulance arriving on the scene. (U.S. Army Air Forces photo)

Same view of the P-39K crash site today showing Don Hinton and Vicki McCurry inspecting some of the crash debris still remaining on the site. (Photo by Dave McCurry)

Don Hinton and Dave McCurry inspect wreckage shortly after the impact site of 42-4394 was discovered. They had been searching for this site for more than three years. (Photo by Vicki McCurry)

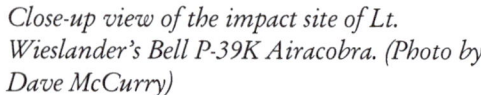

Close-up view of the impact site of Lt. Wieslander's Bell P-39K Airacobra. (Photo by Dave McCurry)

Auxiliary Fuse Box from the left side of the cockpit, in front of the door forward and below the throttle quadrant. (Photo by Dave McCurry)

Cast aluminum piece of engine case from the 12-cylinder Allison V-1710 engine which powered the P-39K. Pieces of the engine were found all over the site. (Photo by Dave McCurry)

Heavy structural part appears to have come from the wing center section of the P-39K. (Photo by Dave McCurry)

Left rudder pedal along with assembly parts were located mid-way along the 500 foot long crash path. (Photo by Dave McCurry)

.50 caliber ammo casings as seen lying about the P-39's crash site. None of the ammo found had been fired, but the projectiles had been removed by kinetic energy created by the crash. (Photo by Dave McCurry)

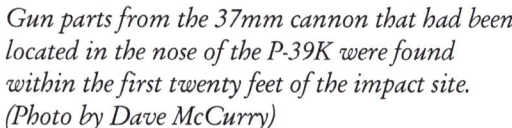

Gun parts from the 37mm cannon that had been located in the nose of the P-39K were found within the first twenty feet of the impact site. (Photo by Dave McCurry)

Large exhaust valve from the P-39's Allison V-1710 engine. (Photo by Dave McCurry)

Don Hinton holds the access panel for the .30 caliber wing gun shell and link ejection ports. (Photo by Dave McCurry)

Close-up view of the shell ejection ports. (Photo by Dave McCurry)

Chapter 21

Blackbird's Night Training Mission Goes Awry

By David L. McCurry

THE Lockheed SR-71 Blackbird is a long-range Mach 3+ strategic reconnaissance aircraft that was operated by the United States Air Force from 1964 through 1998. A total of 32 aircraft were built; 12 were lost in accidents and none were lost to enemy actions. It was developed from the Lockheed A-12 reconnaissance aircraft in the 1960s by Lockheed and its "Skunk Works" division. Aerospace engineer Clarence "Kelly" Johnson was responsible for many of the design's innovative concepts. Many considered this an exotic aircraft made out of exotic materials. The SR-71 was designed to operate at extremely high altitudes and speeds to outrun any kind of threats. If a missile launch was detected, its evasive action was simply to accelerate and outrun the missile. One of the SR-71's interesting designs was its basic stealth characteristics which served as a precursor to future stealth aircraft such as the F-117 stealth fighter and B-2 bomber.

The SR-71 was powered by two Pratt & Whitney J58 turbojet engines and was designed for flight at over Mach 3 with a flight crew in tandem cockpits. The pilot occupied the forward cockpit and the Reconnaissance Systems Officer (RSO) monitored the surveillance systems and equipment from the rear cockpit. The J58 engines were capable of producing a static thrust of 32,500 pounds of thrust each, and the engines were most efficient at around Mach 3.2, the Blackbird's typical cruising speed. At higher speeds the engines largely ceased to produce thrust, and the afterburners then took their place.

SR-71's were painted a dark blue color, almost black, to increase the emission of internal heat and to act as camouflage against the night sky. The black looking color led to its name and call sign "Blackbird." The SR-71 Blackbirds used onboard radar to evade interception efforts, but its greatest protection was its high speed and high altitude capability which made it almost invulnerable to weapons of its day.

Mission Goes Awry

Major Roy L. St. Martin, pilot of Lockheed SR-71A, serial number 61-7965, along with Reconnaissance Systems Officer Captain John A. Carnochan, had completed the requirements of SACM 50-71, "Initial Upgrading Qualification of Aircrew Members SR-71," and were declared combat ready. They were both qualified and current in the SR-71 and were well briefed on the day prior to their flight on a scheduled night time training mission.

In reference to the USAF accident report filed on 8 November 1967, this crew operating SR-71 serial number 61-7965, call sign "ASPEN 28", departed Beale AFB, Marysville, California, at 0058Z on 25 October 1967 for a three hour night training flight. Papa Route consisted of a high-altitude, supersonic leg to Busy Palace air refueling area near Albuquerque, New Mexico, followed by a second climbing acceleration east of Denver, Colorado and return to Beale on a westbound leg north of Salt Lake City, Utah. The flight progressed normally through the air refueling and second acceleration to supersonic cruise. Descent and deceleration from cruise was initiated in the vicinity of Elko, Nevada, approximately two hours and fifteen minutes after takeoff. After completion of checklist item "Throttles retard and set 6300 to 6100 RPM" in the Mach 2.0 checklist, Major St. Martin observed a warning flag on the bank steering bar of the attitude director indicator (ADI).

At this time Major St. Martin also observed that the autopilot had also become disconnected. The ADI showed wings level flight and the horizontal situation indicator (HSI) showed straight, non-turning flight. Because of the warning flag on the ADI steering bar, Major St. Martin switched the attitude reference source to the Flight Reference System (FRS). The ADI showed an immediate unusual attitude of undetermined magnitude, and both the warning flag on the steering bar and the OFF flag on the ADI appeared simultaneously. Major St. Martin advised to Reconnaissance System Officer (RSO), Captain Carnochan, that he had attitude indicator malfunctions and Captain Carnochan confirmed that his astro-inertial navigation system (ANS) had stopped functioning as a valid reference source. Captain Carnochan, on FRS, observed his attitude indicator reflecting a large left wing low, diving turn. Due to the radical attitude displayed in FRS, he stated to Major St. Martin that the FRS was inoperative. However, there were no OFF flags on Captain Carnochan's attitude indicator. Captain Carnochan then switched to ANS and it showed wings level with a constant heading.

The aircraft was on course under control of Salt Lake Center at 0316: 30Z and was at that time directed to Contact Oakland Center. Voice contact was never established, but Oakland Center acquired radar contact at 0316Z and observed the track during the final minutes of flight.

The crew was not aware that the aircraft was making a 180 degree turn towards the east as observed by Oakland Center. The speed had increased to 480 KEAS where Major St. Martin felt that he had stopped the trend of increasing airspeed. Major St. Martin had no outside reference to assist him in the recovery from the unusual attitude because of the darkness. Recovery also could not be effected using the standby attitude indicator.

Major St. Martin directed Captain Carnochan to eject out passing through an estimated 30,000 feet of altitude. Major St. Martin remained with the aircraft for an unknown duration continuing his efforts to recover, but was unsuccessful. Major St. Martin then ejected from the aircraft at an unknown altitude and speed and both crew ejections were successful.

The SR-71 struck the ground at a very high rate of speed in a near vertical dive and was totally destroyed upon impact. The crash occurred at 0320Z in an isolated area with no witnesses at or near the scene of the accident. Total elapsed flight time was estimated to be two hours and twenty minutes.

Analysis of the Accident Scene

Investigators arriving at the crash site of 61-7965 noted that the crater left by the SR-71's impact was of an elliptical shape and measured sixty feet across, corresponding to the 55.6 foot wingspan. A brief post impact fire had been fed by scattered fuel. The undisturbed depth of the crater below the desert floor was eleven feet deep. The site was excavated to a depth of twenty-two feet and produced a consistent distribution of small pieces of internal structure, aircraft skin, and tires. The ground at the site was composed of soft sand and rocks which led to the creation of the large deep crater.

Two pieces of wreckage debris emitted radioactivity five times greater than normal background levels. Disposal of these items was supervised by an authorized representative of the Atomic Energy Commission. All remaining debris was then buried on the site with the approval of the competent authorities.

Board Conclusions

Following the accident investigation of SR-71 61-7965, the flight instrument locations were changed on the entire fleet of SR-71 Blackbirds, and the amended night flight rules required pilots to have at least fifty hours of daytime flying experience in the SR-71s prior to flying night time sorties.

SR-71, 61-7965: Crash Site Today

Today the crash site of Lockheed SR-71A, 61-7965, located 24 nautical miles North of Lovelock, Nevada, appears as a 150 foot wide circular scar with some vegetation and sagebrush growing back. After the investigation was completed years ago, the entire crater containing the remaining debris was bulldozed and smoothed over to fit the contour of the land. There are thousands of tiny fragmented pieces of titanium lying all over the site suggesting that the SR-71 impacted incredibly hard probably turning most of the buried remains of the aircraft into the same thing. Because of the SR-71 being an exotic type of aircraft; that made identifying the small parts very difficult. Some of the notable items found at the site were asbestos-type materials used in the leading edges of the wings for its radar countermeasures to evade interception efforts. Also the nearly black colored paint found on pieces of the titanium skins along with painted-on warning placards which matched those on other SR-71s.

Original Photo of Lockheed SR-71A, serial number 61-7965, as it flies over Beale AFB, CA. (Photo U.S. Air Force)

Today the crash site of SR-71 61-7965, located 24 miles north of Lovelock, Nevada, is a round, bulldozed, one-hundred fifty foot diameter area of disturbed ground. Vegetation has grown back some, and the accident is evidenced by many small pieces if titanium metal littering the ground. (Photo by Dave Trojan)

Many pieces of internal structure like the one in this photo are found throughout the entire crash area. (Photo by Dave Trojan)

Dave Trojan documents small pieces of debris from the SR-71 that he has found in this area. (Photo by Jerry Bowen)

This piece of hinged structure displays a part number for the SR-71. (Photo by Dave Trojan)

Small piece of wreckage from the SR-71 Blackbird displays an easily readable part number for the aircraft. (Photo by Dave Trojan)

Jerry Bowen and Sam Parker standing on the edge of the SR-71's impact crater are surrounded by small parts of the plane. (Photo by Dave Trojan)

Pile of debris shows a variety of skins, composites, and internal structural parts from the SR-71. Most of these items were unidentifiable because the Blackbird is considered an exotic aircraft built with exotic materials. (Photo by Dave Trojan)

This piece of external skin exhibits black paint and part of a painted-on warning marking probably coming from the forward fuselage area. (Photo by Dave Trojan)

Gold colored foil insulation was probably used around oxygen lines in the cockpit area or around engine components. (Photo by Dave Trojan)

Fragments of circuit boards were found to be gold plated and the piece of wiring harness marked MB3J1 was a plug for a circuit board. (Photo by Dave Trojan)

The central portion of the SR-71's impact area shows hundreds of small pieces of titanium scattered all over the ground. (Photo by Dave Trojan)

Chapter 22

Mystery Solved
Super Sabre Found Hundreds Of Miles Off Course

By David L. McCurry

DURING a routine flight, six North American F-100 Super Sabre jet fighter planes departed from Kelly AFB, Texas on July 25, 1957, en route to George AFB, California, via Tucson, Arizona. First Lieutenant Samuel K. Bacon Jr. experienced problems while proceeding in formation and forced the flight to land at Webb AFB, Texas. After a quick turn-around, this included some minor maintenance actions and re-briefing, the flight then took off headed for George AFB. Lt. Bacon was experiencing trouble maintaining formation at 40,000 feet of altitude and acknowledged a change of heading toward Tucson which would be his last transmission. The remaining five aircraft in the flight landed at George AFB without Lt. Bacon whose aircraft was then listed as missing. More than 200 aircraft were involved in searches that lasted for three weeks until the aircraft wreck was finally located 40 miles NNW of Ely, Nevada, on August 20, 1957 with the deceased pilot still in the cockpit.

History of Flight

At approximately 1200 hours on July 25, 1957 the Flight Leader from the 434th Fighter Day Squadron based at George AFB, Victorville, California, conducted a briefing for a flight of six F-100 aircraft to Kelly AFB, Big Springs, Texas, and return to George AFB. The briefing included formation positions, flight route, airfields en route, weather en route, and weather formation flying navigation assignments.

The U.S. Air Force accident report stated that after takeoff at approximately 1300 hours, the flight climbed en route toward Tucson, Arizona, where they received an altitude assignment of 37,000 feet instead of 35,000 feet as had been planned and requested. The flight continued on instruments to Tucson at 37,000 feet in weather until reaching a point east of El Paso, Texas. Shortly after passing El Paso, the flight broke out of the weather and the Flight Leader noticed that Lt. Bacon had taken a position high and in trail of the rest of the formation. While out in the clear, the Flight Leader became unable to locate Lt. Bacon and relayed this information to the rest of the flight group.

Lt. Bacon was soon heard to say something to the affect that he was "getting out." When questioned by the other flight members, he negated his previous statement saying that he was alright and in the clear at 7,000 feet. He then called and said that he thought that his aircraft was on fire, then denied that statement and declared that his heat and vent overheat warning light was on and there were fumes in the cockpit. The Flight Leader directed Lt. Bacon to select the RAM OFF-PRESSURE OFF position on his cockpit pressurization selector and then asked, "How do your gauges read?" Lt. Bacon stated that the warning light had gone out and the gauges read okay.

The Flight Leader advised Lieutenant Bacon to set a course to Wink Radio and climb to 30,000 feet to rendezvous at Wink. The flight, minus Lt. Bacon, proceeded to Wink Radio and entered a port orbit. Lieutenant Bacon apparently flew by mistake to Carlsbad, New Mexico. The Flight Leader then instructed the flight to select UHF Channel #10 for (GCI) control. GCI is an air defense tactic where one or more radar stations or other observation stations are linked to a command communications center which guides interceptor aircraft to an airborne target. GCI site "Fat Chance" established radar contact with all the aircraft and vectored Lt. Bacon to a rendezvous with the others at Wink, fifteen to twenty minutes after he had become lost.

Because of the amount of fuel used during this time, the flight was diverted to Webb AFB, Texas. Over Midland, Texas, the Flight Leader cancelled the instrument (IFR) portion of the Air Route Traffic Control (ARTC) clearance and the flight proceeded to Webb AFB under visual (VFR) conditions and GCI control.

Two aircraft involved with the flight required minor maintenance at Webb AFB which included a tire change and the pumping up of one hydraulic pressure accumulator. During the turn-around, the Flight Leader received a message advising a return to George AFB as soon as possible.

Prior to their departure, Lieutenant Bacon held a lengthy telephone conversation with a friend and was visited by two other friends and their wives. Also during the turn-around time at Webb AFB, The Flight Leader talked with Lt. Bacon about his losing the flight previously. Lt. Bacon said that he had simply lost sight of the leader, and when he looked at his instruments, his attitude gyro was indicating a forty-five degree climbing turn to the right, and he thought his instruments were inoperative. During his attempts to right the aircraft, he said that the airspeed dropped to 110 knots, then built up to Mach 1 just prior to the pull-out. The Flight Leader asked him if he had been in a spin to which Lt. Bacon replied that he wasn't sure what maneuver he had done.

Some of the flight members noted that Lieutenant Bacon appeared not feeling well. He had assured them that he was alright and felt well enough to fly. He had gone to the flight surgeon at 0730 hours that morning complaining of a sore throat. The doctor he had seen made a thorough entry on Lt. Bacon's medical record. The doctor had given Lt. Bacon APCs, and gargle as well as cautioning him against prolonged breathing 100 percent oxygen, as this could cause symptoms of "The Chokes." There was no reason found to ground Lieutenant Bacon.

After determining that each aircraft was equipped with sufficient oxygen, the Flight Leader then briefed the flight group for the return flight to George AFB. The flight positions were to be the same as on the previous leg and the briefing included basic instrument flying, night flying, night formation, vertigo, hypoxia, lost flight procedure, lost wingman procedure, loss of radio, loss of flight instruments, emergency airfields en route, weather en route, emergency GCI procedures, and the flight profile. The Flight Leader further briefed Lt. Bacon on the relative position he should maintain during the return flight. The flight was to consist of two elements of three aircraft each, with a separation of approximately one minute between elements. All flight members had in their possession, flight logs and maps covering the route, which was the reciprocal of the previous route. The entire return flight was to be at 1,000 feet above the overcast.

Weather at the destination for their arrival time was forecast to be fifteen-hundred scattered, visibility four miles in smoke, winds south at eighteen knots with gusts to 28 knots. Weather along the route was forecast to have scattered heavy thunderstorms including heavy icing and turbulence in clouds with the maximum cloud tops of thunderstorms at 49,000 feet.

After a normal take-off at 2041 hours, the flight climbed to 35,000 feet, then to 42,000 feet approaching El Paso. At this time one of the pilots reported to the Flight Leader that his oxygen supply was low, so the first element requested and received ARTC clearance to descend to 38,000 feet then later 34,000 feet. The Flight Leader's element which included Lt. Bacon climbed to 43,000 feet in order to remain 1,000 feet above the overcast. The wingman maintained "fairly close formation" for approximately five minutes, and then Lt. Bacon entered a steep bank toward the element leader and crossed under his aircraft. Moments later Lt. Bacon called that he was crossing and re-crossed back to his original position. The flight Leader could think of no apparent reason for this maneuver and subsequently, Lt. Bacon's formation position varied excessively.

The cloud tops were becoming lower and the Flight Leader called his element to "close in" so as to descend to a lower altitude. After repeating the order and without receiving a response from Lt. Bacon, he immediately observed Lt. Bacon's aircraft dropping slowly out of sight and into the cloud tops. Moments later he heard Lt. Bacon say that he had lost sight of the flight. The Flight Leader then told him the heading, altitude, and airspeed of the element and began a slow descent to 40,000 feet, remaining 1,000 feet, "on top" above the overcast.

Lt. Bacon acknowledged the Flight Leader's instructions to maintain his heading and to descend to 40,000 feet. As the cloud tops continued to lower, the flight descended to 38,000 feet, also acknowledged by Lt. Bacon. Approximately five minutes east of Tucson, two members of the flight engaged afterburners to assist Lt. Bacon in establishing visual contact, but without success. The Flight Leader again transmitted heading, altitude, and airspeed information and instructed Lt. Bacon to advise when he had a compass swing on Tucson Radio indicating that he had passed the station fix. Lt. Bacon acknowledged the transmission and at 2043 hours, the Flight Leader passed over the Tucson Radio fix with Lt. Bacon reporting soon afterward that he also had a compass swing on Tucson. The Flight Leader then instructed him to turn to a heading of 284 degrees for Gila Bend Radio and again, Lt. Bacon acknowledged that transmission. That was the last transmission heard from Lt. Bacon.

Advised by Tucson Radio that Gila Bend Radio was not transmitting, The Flight Leader transmitted this information "in the blind" for Lt. Bacon. He then contacted GCI site "HAMMER" then "STANLEY" on UHF Channel #10, for radar assistance in rejoining his element. However, "STANLEY" did not establish radar contact with Lt. Bacon's aircraft, although strong "radar paints" were returned on the Flight Leader's aircraft. "STANLEY" searched in front of and seventy miles behind the Flight Leader's aircraft with both height and search radar. The Battle Staff Officer on duty at "STANLEY" at the time stated that he earnestly believed that had Lt. Bacon been in the air at the time he searched the area, an indication would have been present on the director's scope.

With there being nothing further that he could do at this point, the Flight Leader proceeded to George AFB and landed at approximately 2135 hours, five minutes behind the first element.

Expressing their faith that 1st Lieutenant Samuel K. Bacon was still alive, Lt. Bacon's father, Dr. Samuel K. Bacon Sr. from Hollywood, California, along with Lt. Bacon's wife, Doris May Bacon, posted a $2,500.00 reward for locating Lt. Bacon. It was strongly believed the Lt. Bacon had either survived a forced landing or parachuted to safety. Lt. Bacon's beautiful honey-blonde haired wife, Mrs. Doris Bacon, along with Lt. Bacon's six month old daughter, Debra Lyn, came to the Biltmore Hotel where they lived in Victorville, California, to meet the press and restate an offer of $2500 reward for the location and rescue of Lt. Bacon. She also exhibited samples of posters which a number of companies were distributing to flyers, prospectors, miners, explorers, and other travelers in the area where Lt. Bacon's plane disappeared. Doris stated that Lt. Bacon was what the Air Force called a "cool cookie"... trained to get himself out of tough situations. Over the course of several weeks, Lt. Bacon's father had received thousands of letters and a number of clues regarding the missing plane to no avail. Telephone calls and letters from all parts of the world were received by the family expressing that they were praying for Lt. Bacon's safety.

Lt. and Mrs. Bacon had met at Brigham Young University where they were both enrolled. Eventually they were married in the Salt Lake Temple in Salt Lake City, Utah. The young twenty-eight year old pilot, a native of Hollywood, had previously served for two and one-half years on a Netherlands Mission, and then toured the world with his parents before returning home to continue his education. Doris Bacon's parents, Mr. and Mrs. James Rasband, were from Seattle, Washington.

Lieutenant Bacon and his aircraft were listed as missing until the aircraft, with the pilot still in the cockpit, was located and positively identified 40 miles north-northwest of Ely, Nevada on August 20, 1957. The nearly intact jet had been spotted by a private construction company pilot who had reported that the wings were still intact with the cockpit section burned out. According to the accident report; the post-crash fire was fueled mainly by a rupture of the Liquid Oxygen Converter with escaping oxygen increasing the intensity of the cockpit fire.

The cause of this sad tragic accident was determined as unknown by the investigation committee but was thought to have been caused by oxygen deprivation from a cockpit oxygen problem which rendered the pilot either unconscious or having passed away. An oxygen/pressurization system failure causing hypoxia (deficiency in the amount of oxygen) to the pilot was not uncommon at that time. Lt. Bacon had reported fumes in the cockpit and selected the RAM OFF- PRESSURE OFF position on his cockpit pressurization selector. Hypoxia was suspected due to his physiological problems and slow communications with other members of the flight. The F-100 required the pilots to be on 100 % oxygen all the time because of possible fumes in the cockpit. The liquid oxygen system used a pressure demand mask and a converter to breathable oxygen in the cockpit. The jet was flying at over 30,000 feet and without oxygen, the pilot would have blacked out. The aircraft flew on for hundreds of miles, off course, before running out of fuel and crashing into mountains north-northwest of Ely, Nevada.

Lt. Bacon's sister, Cherilyn Eager, stated in a letter that fifty-seven years later, on April 6, 2014, Doris had passed away. She was honored to attend her funeral service on May 10, 2014 along with Lt. Bacon's daughter Debbie and her husband Len. Also in attendance were his granddaughters and great-granddaughters.

Years later after the crash of Lt. Bacon's plane; Cherilyn heard her own mother's soft cries from her bedroom. Cherilyn walked in and asked if she was okay. She said she was fine, "just missing my son."

What Cherilyn's brother's death had taught her was; to the many mothers and fathers who have lost their sons and daughters for this "great cause" and are still "just missing them" today: Thank you, and may the Lord bring you peace and comfort.

F-100, 54-2090: Crash Site Today

On a recent visit to the Pequop Mountain Range southeast of Wells, Nevada to help build a Memorial Monument at the crash site of a Boeing B-47 Stratojet Bomber, we also visited the crash site of Lieutenant Samuel K. Bacon's North American F-100 Super Sabre, serial number 54-2090, which is located a one hour drive south of there. The site is located ten miles west of a small ghost town called Cherry Creek, Nevada, on the western slope of the Egan Mountain Range. We were able to drive gravel roads to within a one-half mile hike through the mountains which was a blessing considering temperatures in the 90s above an elevation of 8,000 feet. There was a large rock outcropping located just below the wreck which caused us to have to navigate uphill to get around it, but not too bad of a hike.

Our hiking group included Dave Trojan, Sam Parker, Don Hinton, as well as Dave and Vicki McCurry. On arrival to the site, it appeared as though the wreck was mostly intact, but on closer inspection, it was obvious that a portable smelter had been to work on salvaging some of the aluminum from the wreck. Because of the difficulty of salvagers hauling material out, there is still quite a bit left though. Now that the wreck is more than fifty years old, it now falls within the antiquities protection law.

Both wings are mostly intact, and the entire engine along with some of the rear empennage is still there, but the vertical stabilizer and front portion of the fuselage is missing. Both drop tanks which we figured might still be at the site are missing, presumably recovered by the salvagers. We also took note that the main landing gears were in the retracted position along with the nose gear laying separate. All three landing gears had obviously been involved in the burned out section of the plane. On close inspection of the Pratt & Whitney J57-P-21 turbojet engine; we noticed evidence confirming that it was not producing power at all when the Super Sabre jet crashed. While standing next to Lt. Bacon's wrecked plane, one can't help but to ponder the bizarre events leading to this tragic accident.

The North American Aviation F-100 Super Sabre, powered by a Pratt & Whitney J-57-21 turbojet engine, was capable of supersonic speed in level flight. Nicknamed the "Hun" short for one-hundred, it flew the most missions during the Vietnam War, flying extensively over South Vietnam as the Air Force's primary close air support jet. It made its first flight on May 25, 1953 and served with the USAF from 1954 through 1971. (Photo U.S. Air Force)

First Lieutenant Samuel Kenneth Bacon, Jr. (Photo Courtesy of Cherilyn Eagar)

First Lieutenant Samuel Kenneth Bacon, Jr.

Original Accident Report photo of Lt. Bacon's wrecked North American F-100 Super Sabre, serial number 54-2090. (Photo U.S. Air Force)

The crash site of F-100 Super Sabre 54-2090 as it appears today. The retracted nose gear assembly removed by scrappers can be seen in the left center of the photo. (Photo by Dave McCurry)

Dave Trojan sits near the F-100's Pratt & Whitney J57-P-21 turbojet engine with one of the aircraft's main landing gears in view. (Photo by Dave McCurry)

Ejection seat rails and rear armor plating from the wrecked F-100 sit nearby. (Photo by Dave McCurry)

Our wreck hunting group which includes from left; Don Hinton, Sam Parker, Dave McCurry, and Dave Trojan as we are assembled around the F-100's J-57 engine just prior to departing the site. (Photo by Don Hinton)

Vivid red, white, and blue paint colors of the national star and bar insignia on the underside of the aircraft's right wing. (Photo by Don Hinton)

Author Dave McCurry inspects the faded insignia on the F-100's left wing. (Photo by Vicki McCurry)

Members of our hiking group as they go about documenting and taking photos of the Super Sabre wreck. (Photo by Dave McCurry)

Remains of the F-100's rear empennage as it rests on the left wing. (Photo by Dave McCurry)

Both wings and the retracted main landing gears from the F-100 Super Sabre with Vicki McCurry and Don Hinton in the background finishing their photo survey. (Photo by Dave McCurry)

Right wing from the F-100 still shows a faded USAF marking. (Photo by Dave McCurry)

Don Hinton and Vicki McCurry inspect the remains of Lt. Bacon's North American F-100 Super Sabre, serial number 54-2090, one last time before we started our hike back out of the mountains. (Photo by Dave McCurry)

Chapter 23

Inclement Weather: A Trap for a Vultee BT-13

By David L. McCurry

ON April 29, 1947, a Canadian registered Vultee BT-13 on a flight from Kellogg, Idaho, to Coeur d'Alene, Idaho, crashed high in the mountains northeast of Coeur d'Alene killing both occupants aboard. The war surplus aircraft with a Canadian registration number of C56962 had hit high trees in poor weather before plummeting into the snow covered forest. The two occupants, James Fisher, an oil company superintendent from Wallace, Idaho, and Harvey Meacham, a garage superintendent from Kellogg, Idaho, both survived the initial accident with burns and severe injuries, but succumbed to their injuries while attempting to find help. One of the two men had staggered a quarter of a mile to a logging road while the other was found 500 feet from the wreckage. The wreck was discovered four days later by loggers working in the area.

BT-13: Crash Site Today

Today the war surplus wreck of Vultee C56962 lies deeply hidden in the heavily wooded Coeur d'Alene National Forest, and choked off by thick underbrush. A good portion of one wing is still there, but the tail section and some of the outer fuselage skin is missing, probably salvaged. The tube steel frame, firewall, and a good portion of cockpit items are still there. The engine was either salvaged or rolled down the mountain for quite a distance, but couldn't be located after searching the area for 300 yards downhill. There was also quite a bit of fire evidence in the forward fuselage area. This mountainous area has acquired quite a few aircraft wrecks in the past with most of them being civilian.

The Vultee BT-13 Valiant nicknamed the "Vultee Vibrator" was an American World War Two era basic trainer, built by Vultee Aircraft for the United States Army Air Corps. The BT-13 was first introduced in June 1940, and was powered by a 450 hp Pratt & Whitney R-985 nine cylinder radial engine. 9,525 units were built. (U.S. Air Force)

A large section of the wing from the wrecked BT-13 with elk hunter Eric Lund standing in the background. (Photo by Marc McDonald)

Another view of the Vultee BT-13's wing section. (Photo by Marc McDonald)

Fire damage seen on this electrical box which was mounted in the front cockpit. (Photo by Marc McDonald)

A piece of the BT-13's windscreen found near the wreck. (Photo by Marc McDonald)

"Vultee" rudder pedal as seen in the rear cockpit. (Photo by Marc McDonald)

View of the BT-13's front cockpit area with the throttle/mixture controls at left and the toggle switch panel on the right. The fuel tank selector and battery switch are in the upper center of the photo. (Photo by Marc McDonald)

Tube steel frame of the BT-13 from where the tail was attached with this view looking toward the front of the aircraft. (Photo by Marc McDonald)

Piece of cast aluminum with a "74" prefix on the part number indicates a Vultee BT-13A type aircraft. (Photo by Marc McDonald)

Marc McDonald holding green painted fuselage skin stands next to the front cockpit area and engine firewall of the BT-13 with part of the aircraft's windscreen resting on it. (Photo by Marc McDonald)

Prop pitch control from the BT-13's front cockpit. (Photo by Marc McDonald)

Throttle and mixture controls located in the front cockpit. (Photo by Marc McDonald)

Chapter 24

Snow Storm Dooms B-25 On Mt. Timpanogos

By David L. McCurry

ON 9 March 1955 a USAF North American TB-25H, serial number 44-30050, departed Great Falls Air Force Base, Montana, en route to March Air Force Base, California. Aboard the B-25 were: Major Daniel C. Howley (instructor pilot); 2nd Lieutenant Howard E. St. John Jr. (copilot); Airman 2C Doyle Dempsey (engineer); and two civilian engineers working for the Air Force, Donald R. Cubbage and Maurice McNulty. The first two legs of this flight with landings at Ellsworth Air Force Base, South Dakota, and again at Hill Air Force Base, Utah, were uneventful.

After landing at Hill AFB, the B-25 was refueled with 972 gallons of fuel and was the only aircraft serviced. The crew and passengers had a small meal at a snack bar adjacent to the Base Operations and were in a hurry to continue the flight. The aircraft apparently had oxygen but the copilot's conversation with the weather forecaster indicated that there was only one oxygen mask available.

At about 1815 MST copilot St. John requested a weather briefing from the base weather forecaster. Their route would include a flight plan to March AFB via A2 Airway to Summit Intersection and B-14 Airway to Riverside, California. After receiving the weather briefing, he informed pilot Howley that the flight could not be conducted under VFR (Visual Flight Rules) conditions. Major Howley appeared to be upset over the prospect of an IFR (Instrument Flight Rules) flight and requested to be briefed by the forecaster on the expected weather en route. Maj. Howley stated to the forecaster that he had planned to go to March AFB and return to Great Falls AFB in VFR conditions all in the same night. The weather forecaster informed both Maj. Howley and Lt. St. John that the average forecast wind over their route was 240 degrees at 25 knots, with 30 knots in the Salt Lake Valley. Later that evening at 2000 MST, Hill AFB had indicated winds at 12,000 feet being 250 degrees at 43 knots.

Maj. Howley filed IFR, 12,000 feet via A2 Airway to Summit Intersection and B14 Airway to Riverside, California. Before leaving operations Howley was advised that there would be about a thirty minute delay in obtaining an (ARTC) Air Route Traffic Control clearance for the flight. He then requested a briefing on an instrument departure from the Airdrome Officer. Maj. Howley received a phone call from the Airdrome Officer who had previously advised Lt. St. John that there was no specific briefing for an instrument takeoff from Hill AFB. Depending on traffic, the ARTC Center at Salt Lake City probably would require a climb on course, or to climb on the west leg of the Ogden LF Range and depart that station at an assigned altitude.

The Hill AFB tower cleared the B-25 to a taxiway for engine run-up and advised that takeoff would be on runway 25. After the run-up was completed, there was a delay of approximately forty to fifty minutes in receiving their ARTC clearance. From the tower transcript, it was apparent that Maj. Howley had become very irked during this delay. When the clearance was finally received, Howley had some difficulty in copying it correctly. He acknowledged that he was cleared via A2 to Summit Intersection, B14 to Riverside, and to maintain 12,000 feet and climb on course. Maj. Howley was advised that the time limit was about to expire and was requested to expedite his takeoff on Runway 25. While trying to hurry, he erroneously lined up on a taxiway headed northwest. After taxiing into position on Runway 25, Howley was then cleared for takeoff at 1932 MST.

At 1937 MST, the aircraft reported over Salt Lake City LF Radio at 9,000 feet. Maj. Howley did not report whether he was climbing and gave an estimate of 1948 MST to Fairfield Radio which was the next radio fix at thirty-four nautical miles along the route. Fairfield was not a compulsory reporting point and had no voice facilities. Salt Lake City Radio acknowledged the position and the estimate. The position of the aircraft directly over the Salt Lake City LF Radio at 1937 was verified by both the Salt Lake City municipal airport tower on their radar scope and also Approach Control. Due to other traffic, the operator did not track the B-25 after it passed the Range Station. This was the last radio transmission heard from B-25H, 44-30050.

INVESTIGATION CONCLUSIONS

It was later determined that the B-25 aircraft actually maintained VFR conditions from takeoff until passing Salt Lake City Radio. The aircraft was below the overcast when passing Salt Lake City Radio, and then shortly afterward flew into a solid overcast. Maj. Howley may have had some difficulty maintaining radio contact due to precipitation static and may have encountered light rime icing. Whether he encountered any mechanical difficulties was never determined. The aircraft had drifted fifteen miles to the east of the centerline of the airway, and may have encountered moderate to severe turbulence before impacting the mountains at approximately 1950 MST.

Wreckage of the B-25 was found by a search plane at approximately 1645 MST the following day at the 11,100 foot elevation on a shelf of the northern side of Mt. Timpanogos. The plane had crashed in a level attitude six-hundred feet below the summit of the mountain in deep snow. A mountain climbing group struggling in waist deep snow, whom was continuously threatened by avalanches, arrived at the crash site three days later only to find there were no survivors. With the depth of the snow on the mountain top being nine feet deep, much of the wreckage was buried and only four of the five bodies could be found. Two feet of snow had fallen on the mountain since the accident had occurred making it that much more difficult to inspect wreckage and find the fifth body. The fifth body was reportedly not recovered until May 28, 1955. The Forest Service had blocked public access to the mountain until the last body had been recovered.

TB-25H, 44-30050: CRASH SITE TODAY

The crash site of TB-25H, 44-30050, is located on the northern side of Mt. Timpanogos near the city of Pleasant Grove, Utah. Today the site located on a rocky shelf at an elevation of 11,100 feet still contains a relatively large amount of the remains of the aircraft. Parts of the B-25 that can easily be identified include both of the 1,700 horsepower Wright R-2600 Cyclone radial engines, landing gears, wing panels, and one of the B-25's vertical stabilizers. The popular hike to the crash site is fairly steep and requires an all-day round trip, but is well worth the mountain air and spectacular views.

The North American TB-25N in this photo taken in 1956 was assigned to the Missouri Air National Guard and was very similar to TB-25H, serial number 44-30050, which crashed on Mt. Timpanogos, Utah, 9 March 1955. (U.S. Air Force Photo)

Today the remains of TB-25H, 44-30050, can be found on a rocky shelf at an elevation of 11,100 feet on the northern side of Mt. Timpanogos. Note one of the aircraft's engines sitting on a cliff in the center of the photo. (Photo by Kristy McCurry)

One of the main landing gears from the TB-25H. (Photo by Kristy McCurry)

Several large fuselage panels like the one pictured were noted at the crash site. (Photo by Kristy McCurry)

Caleb McCurry inspects one of the 1,700 horsepower Wright Cyclone radial engines from the crashed TB-25H. (Photo by Kristy McCurry)

One of the B-25's twin vertical stabilizers on Mt. Timpanogos. (Photo by Kristy McCurry)

Part of the Air Force serial number ending in "050" can clearly be seen on the vertical stabilizer from the B-25. (Photo by Kristy McCurry)

Caleb McCurry stands amongst piles of debris from the crashed B-25 on Mt. Timpanogos. (Photo by Kristy McCurry)

Inside view of a piece of a fuselage panel from the TB-25H. (Photo by Kristy McCurry)

One of the B-25's engines sits next to a piece of wing panel. (Photo by Kristy McCurry)

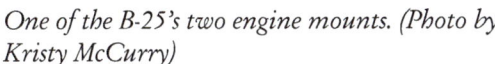

One of the B-25's two engine mounts. (Photo by Kristy McCurry)

Wing panels along with a wing flap sit in a pile at the crash site of B-25H, 44-30050. (Photo by Kristy McCurry)

Chapter 25

Phantom Jet Disappears On Routine Training Mission

By David L. McCurry

MAJOR Carleton K. Sprague, a 1951 West Point graduate and veteran of World War II and Korea, was stationed at Mountain Home Air Force Base, Idaho, from March 1963 until his disappearance on November 12, 1970. He had also served a one year tour in Thailand and Vietnam from 1966 through 1967 and was credited with 258 combat flying missions mostly over North Vietnam. He was awarded eleven Air Medals, two Distinguished Flying Crosses, and the Air Force Commendation Medal.

Flying an RF-4C Phantom II reconnaissance plane; Maj. Sprague had been shot at many times but his Phantom jet could easily outrun the Russian built Mig fighter planes. He had never been hit but many in his squadron had been. Having no armament Maj. Sprague couldn't fight, but would wait when he spotted a Mig, and if the Mig sighted him and committed himself, Maj. Sprague would leave rapidly.

Planning for missions usually required three or four hours of time after being assigned a target. Daytime missions were flown visually and factors on how high they flew depended on the target's defenses. For night missions, they flew totally by radar. He would tell the back-seater (the pilot systems operator or navigator) how he wanted to approach a target, and then the systems operator would decide on his best course. The types of targets would be anything from bridges to steel mills, depots, railroads, or communications routes, anything that was a target of military value.

MISSING AIRCREW

Major Sprague, of Bangor, Maine, along with his navigator, Captain Terrence M. Andrews, from Sacramento, California, had taken off in a McDonnell-Douglas RF-4C Phantom II reconnaissance plane, serial number 65-0860, for a routine training mission on the morning of November 12, 1970, from Mountain Home AFB and disappeared. They were assigned to the 67th Tactical Reconnaissance Wing based at Mountain Home AFB, Mountain Home, Idaho.

The training mission was planned to be conducted over Southern Idaho, Western Utah, Northern Nevada, and Western Wyoming. The search for the aircraft covered more than 100,000 square miles of the four-state area and involved aircraft from Mountain Home AFB, units and personnel from the Civil Air Patrol, Air National Guard, Air Force Reserve, and Western Aerospace Rescue and Recovery Service from Hamilton AFB, California. While flying on instruments in a snow storm, the Phantom II had struck an 8,000 ft. ridge top near Oakley, Idaho, destroying the aircraft and killing both men aboard.

Wreckage of the Phantom jet was located seven months later by Ron Perish of Burley, Idaho, a rancher who was repairing a fence in the mountains south of Oakley, Idaho. He had also found two bodies and personal equipment bearing the names of the missing crewmen. Wreckage was spread over an area approximately 250 yards long, and had been covered by snow which had just recently melted.

RF-4C, 65-0860: CRASH SITE TODAY

Not much remains today at the crash site of the RF-4C Phantom II reconnaissance jet located near Oakley, Idaho, other than the memory of what had happened there forty-five years ago. There are small bits and pieces of aluminum from 65-0860 scattered over an area several hundred yards long, but nothing real identifiable.

Visiting the site gives one a somber realization of the ultimate price that our military pilots sometimes pay, but it also makes one respect the price paid in allowing us our freedoms; something we should never take for granted. As time moves forward, sadly part of our history is quickly forgotten, but we should never forget the names and the important missions guided by our military personnel who continue to pay that price, which ultimately gives us the freedom to live in the greatest country on earth.

The McDonnell Douglas RF-4C Phantom II was an unarmed photographic reconnaissance version of the USAF's F-4C which carried a variety of film-based and side-looking radar sensors for the Air Force. They made their debut in Vietnam on 30 October 1965, flying the hazardous post-strike reconnaissance missions. (U.S. Air Force)

Major Carleton K. Sprague at an early age sits in the cockpit of a Lockheed F-80 Shooting Star jet fighter plane. Note the name of his wife Sara painted on the nose. (Photo courtesy of Carole Quallio)

Maj. Sprague standing on the ladder leading to the cockpit of an RF-4C Phantom II reconnaissance plane. Other person in the photo was unidentified. (Photo courtesy of Carole Quallio)

Box of crash debris collected by Maj. Sprague's son when visiting the RF-4C crash site near Oakley, Idaho. (Photo courtesy of Carole Quallio)

Major Carleton Sprague's helmet, watch, ring, and dog tags were recovered by the USAF from the RF-4C crash site. (Photo courtesy of Carole Quallio)

Maj. Sprague was buried in Alabama. Photo is of his headstone. (Photo courtesy of Carole Quallio)

Reverse side of an airframe part from the RF-4C crash site. (Photo by Marc McDonald)

Large piece of rubber which looks like it could be part of a fuel bladder. (Photo by Marc McDonald)

Pile of debris placed on a rock probably by someone who had previously walked the crash site. (Photo by Marc McDonald)

Piece of an electronic circuit board. (Photo by Marc McDonald)

Large hinge maybe from a landing gear door or access panel found at the RF-4C wreck. (Photo by Marc McDonald)

Data plate off of some type of hydraulic device. (Photo by Marc McDonald)

Several bent-up engine turbine blades were found at the site. (Photo by Marc McDonald)

Broken piece of the radio call sign found at the RF-4C crash site led to discovering all of the details of the crash. (Photo by Marc McDonald)

This item appeared to be part of a fuel tank selector valve. (Photo by Marc McDonald)

Chapter 26

Regina Airlines DC-3: Attempt at VFR Flight Proves Fatal

By David L. McCurry

WORKERS manning two fire lookout towers near Vail, Washington, on the night of September 1, 1953, reported seeing two flashes followed by the sound of an explosion. What they had witnessed at about 7:00 p.m., was the moment that a chartered transport plane on a domestic non-scheduled passenger flight had crashed in the Cascade Mountains.

All 21 persons aboard were killed which included nineteen enlisted army soldiers from Fort Ord California, and two crewmembers. The soldiers were believed to have been flying north for assignments overseas.

The Regina Cargo Airlines Douglas DC-3, registration number N19941, had departed Monterey-Fort Ord AFB, California, at 2:08 p.m. en route to McChord Air Force Base, Washington, and it was last heard from over Portland, Oregon, 4 hours and 12 minutes later. Shortly afterward it was noted to be overdue at McChord. A wide search had been started that night in Lewis County, but was hampered by low clouds in the area.

After hearing reports of the missing plane on the radio the following morning; two employees from the Weyerhaeuser Timber Co. went searching for the missing DC-3 and eventually found the plane's wreckage by following the smell of smoke.

The Regina Airlines DC-3 had plowed through high trees on a mountain ridge 26 miles short of its McChord destination. The transport plane had struck the ridge at a 3,000 foot elevation scattering small debris along the top and down the backside of the ridge.

Most of the larger pieces of wreckage came to rest in wet underbrush along the top side of a canyon. After burning on impact, the only recognizable portion left was the silver tail with a red stripe running through it. A Weyerhaeuser bulldozer was used to clear a road for vehicles to park within 60 yards the crash site, but foot access the rest of the way to the site was considered torture in the thick wet underbrush. The trees and brush were so dense that the site could only be seen from about 30 yards away. The bodies were removed to Vail, and then on to McChord Air Force Base.

PROBABLE CAUSE

The DC-3, chartered by the army, was on an Instrument Flight Rules (IFR) flight plan which was cancelled at 6:20 p.m. on the night of the accident. The probable cause of the accident was considered to be the pilot's attempt to continue the flight under Visual Flight Rules (VFR) during instrument conditions.

Those onboard included:

Capt. Eugene Jones (Pilot)
G. W. Dorsett (Co-pilot)
Sgt. John Davis, Jr.
Pvt. Rojelio Nunez
Cpl. Raymond C. Silver, Jr.
S. 1. Gustav F. Wickiloren
Cpl. Henry T. Zimmerman
Pvt. Joseph M. Briscoe
Pvt. Carl C. Butler
Pvt. Albert Davis
Pvt. Ezekiel Turk, Jr.
Pfc. Charles A. Gale
Pfc. Willie L. Lenell
Cpl. Ted K. Matsuyoshi
Pfc. Freeman O. Montgomery
Pfc. Jose N. Ruelas
Cpl. Lloyd L. Stanlake
S. 1. Henry L. Foss
Pvt. Joseph Gaynard, Jr.
Pvt. William R. Mohr
Cpl. Leamon E. Schulz

REGINA CARGO AIRLINES DC-3: CRASH SITE TODAY

The crash site of the Regina Cargo Airlines DC-3, registration number N19941, is located on Weyerhaeuser Timber Company land, approximately twelve miles southeast of Vail, Washington, in the rugged Cascade Mountains. The DC-3 had hit tall trees along the top of a high ridge line, disintegrating as it cut a swath through the trees, then scattering small pieces of wreckage along and over the back side of the ridge and into a canyon.

Today many small parts of the plane, spread out over a one-half acre area, can be found entangled in heavy brush and old-growth timber. The engines and all large parts of the aircraft were probably salvaged years ago, leaving mostly small shards of aluminum at the crash site. The largest pieces of remaining debris range in size from two or three feet in length. Most of the wreckage left at the site includes parts from the wings and fuselage, along with interior parts and seat frames. It is interesting to see shards of metal still embedded into the old-growth timber. A sobering view is that of the many personal items which were left behind after the crash site clean-up years ago. Looking through the field of debris one can find boots, shoes, remains of duffel bags, miscellaneous cargo items, rotten seat belt material, and belt buckles. That makes this kind of a tragedy really hit home. If the plane had only missed the trees on the top of this last ridge, it would have no doubt arrived safely at McChord Air Force Base.

The Douglas DC-3 nicknamed "Gooney Bird" was first introduced in 1936. With a speed of 207 mph and a range of 1,500 miles, it revolutionized air travel in the 1930s and 1940s. 16,079 variants of the DC-3/C-47 were built and after 80 years of service, approximately 400 are still flying today. (Photo by Dave McCurry)

During the first twenty years of its existence, the 21 seat DC-3 was a major contribution to airline service worldwide, and the military version of this aircraft (C-47 Skytrain) was used extensively during World War II especially for dropping paratroopers and towing gliders during the D-Day Invasion. Later on, the now surplus DC-3s and C-47s were used as cargo planes such as this SALAIR Airlines DC-3 seen taxiing on the airport ramp in Pasco, Washington in the latter 1980s. (Photo by Dave McCurry)

John Barone lifts what appears to be part of the underside of a wing from the Regina Cargo Airlines DC-3 which crashed near Vail, Washington, on September 1, 1953. (Photo by Jim Ward)

Some of the larger pieces of wreckage from the Regina Airlines DC-3, registration number N19941, which still exist at the crash site today. (Photo by Jim Ward)

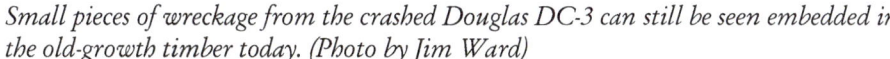

Small pieces of wreckage from the crashed Douglas DC-3 can still be seen embedded in the old-growth timber today. (Photo by Jim Ward)

Another view of a piece of the crashed DC-3's wing structure. (Photo by Jim Ward)

Jim Ward documents pieces of wreckage from the Regina Airlines DC-3. Note the thick growth in the forest which made finding and examining parts of the wreck a bit of a challenge. (Photo by John Barone)

Chapter 27

The Dakota Crewmen of Sulphur Mountain

By Cye Laramie

ENTERING production in January of 1942, a month after the attack on Pearl Harbor, the Douglas C-47 Skytrain rapidly gained status as the best military transport of World War II. Derived from the DC-3 passenger plane which began flying in 1935, the C-47 had a strengthened rear fuselage area and cargo doors. The redesigned aircraft could carry jeeps or small trucks and the new metal bench seats could accommodate 28 armed paratroops. The Skytrains were also equipped with more powerful 1200 horsepower Pratt and Whitney engines. More than 1000 C-47s were used on the eve of the D-Day invasion to drop troops and equipment behind enemy lines. The C-47 Skytrains that went to the Royal Air Force were renamed "Dakotas", many of which were sent to Canada for training purposes. C-47 Dakota FZ-583 was assigned to the 32nd Operational Training Unit at Comox Air Field, Vancouver Island, Canada, on January 9th, 1944.

On the evening of June 26th, 1945, Dakota FZ-583 took off from Comox on a night training mission. Piloting the aircraft was 20 year old Sgt. Daniel Victor Sorfleet, son of Victor W. and Alice Sorfleet from Horncastle, Lincolnshire, England. The young pilot had received his wings a month prior to this flight. Serving as co-pilot was 23 year old P/O John Charles Eric Bayston, son of Arthur S. and Lillian J. Bayston from Holbeach, Lincolnshire, England. P/O Bayston had been married shortly before being sent to Canada for training. The navigator on the flight was 23 year old Sgt. Charles Arthur John Wilton, son of Arthur E. and Harriet A. Wilton of Stubbington, Hampshire, England. Before volunteering for the RAF Reserve, Sgt. Wilton had been a police constable at Portsmouth, Hampshire. Like Sgt. Sorfleet, P/O Bayston and Sgt. Wilton had received their training the previous month.

As the sun sank in the west, Dakota FZ-583 and her newly trained, inexperienced crew thundered off into history and would not be seen again for over eight years.

Although the exact flight path the aircrew had taken is unknown, it is most likely that they were circumnavigating Vancouver Island in a counter clockwise direction. Their last radio contact was most likely made over the west coast of Vancouver Island since this was the initial search area after FZ-583 failed to return to base. During the intensive search effort, three other aircraft that had been missing for several months were located but there was no sign of the missing Dakota and her crew of three. After an exhaustive two week effort, the search was called off and the families of the three crewmen were notified that their loved ones were missing.

Following the end of World War II, the logging industry in the Pacific NW began to grow substantially due to a housing boom as the veterans of the war came home and started families. This required many new forestry roads to be built into previously inaccessible areas for the harvest of old growth timber. One of these roads was built up the Suiattle River in Snohomish County. By 1952 this road had been punched in as far as Sulphur Creek at the foot of Sulphur Mountain. Besides timber, this road exposed the upper river area to hunting and recreational use.

In September of 1953, three hunters from the Vaughn and Allyn, Washington area, decided to take advantage of the newly accessible forest land and planned a goat hunt on Sulphur Mountain. The three men, Wes Davidson, Don Miller, and Harold Cleveland, were hardy woodsmen with years of back woods experience.

As the three men climbed up and over the top of Sulphur Mountain on the morning of September 15th, they came across something totally unexpected; the remains of some sort of aircraft scattered across the mountainside. After first finding an engine, propeller, and wheel, the trail of debris led them to the shattered fuselage and wings of an aircraft painted in brown and green military camouflage. In the tangle of metal debris were the skeletal remains of at least two men. Also found was a medical kit with the faded letters "RCAF" printed on it. Having no clue as to what type of aircraft they had found, the three hunters made a few mental notes as they headed back down the mountain to report their find to the US Coast Guard.

Since they had only found one engine, the hunters initially reported to the Coast Guard that the plane was a single engine military aircraft with possible ties to the RCAF. The Coast Guard in return, reported the find to both the Canadian and United States Air Forces, both of whom denied it was one of their aircraft. The USAF agreed to investigate the wreckage in an attempt to solve the mystery.

On Tuesday, Oct. 13th, Sgt. Talbert from McChord Air Field's Rescue Squadron arrived at Darrington by helicopter and was driven to Sulphur Creek Camp where he began the ascent up Sulphur Mountain taking the same route as the hunters did several weeks earlier. Upon arriving at the crash site, he did a thorough search of the wreckage and was able to identify the aircraft as RCAF Dakota FZ-583. He was also able to make a positive identification of at least one of the victims. Sgt. Talbert then gathered up as many of the crewmen's bones as he could locate and buried them in a cairn near the wreckage. He then returned to Darrington and was flown back to McChord Field by helicopter.

From here the story takes another sad turn. What really happened is unclear but the fact is, the families of Daniel Sorfleet, John Bayston, and Charles Wilton, were never informed that they had been found. Being that the Canadian Government had on file a record that stated Dakota FZ-583 had crashed on Sulphur Mountain, there can be no doubt that McChord Field officials had done their job of reporting the information to the Canadian Government. For whatever the reason, the families of the three crewmen continued to believe their loved ones were still missing decades after they had actually been found. The parents of the three men lived out their lives and sadly passed away never learning the truth.

In May of 2002, P/O John C. E. Bayston's sister wrote to the Comox Air Force Museum seeking any information that might be available about her brother's disappearance. To her astonishment the return letter from the Museum brought the news that her brother's aircraft had been found nearly fifty years earlier on a mountain in Washington State.

My involvement in this case began in February of 2014, when I was forwarded an email from Ally Ellis of Lincolnshire, England asking for help in finding information on a plane crash on Sulphur Mountain in Washington State. It turned out that Ally was the niece of the pilot, Sgt. Daniel V. Sorfleet, and she had learned, through her own research in 2012, that his aircraft, Dakota FZ-583, had been found after being missing for a period of eight years. She went on to say that the families of the three crewmen had never been informed that the aircraft wreck had been located or that the three men had been buried on the mountainside. After some thought, I decided to take on this new project and began doing research.

I already knew about a plane wreck on Sulphur Mountain from a story told by a hiker who had stumbled upon it fifteen years earlier. Luckily, this man had taken a couple photos of the wreckage, including a photo of the landing gear, and drawn a map of the wreckage area. I had copies of both in my possession. From the photo I was able to determine that the landing gear was that of a Douglas DC-3/C-47 aircraft. Unfortunately, about this same time I also learned that the road to the Sulphur Mountain area on the Suiattle River had washed out eight years earlier and was never repaired resulting in an eight to ten mile bicycle ride just to get to the trailhead.

RCAF DAKOTA FZ-583: CRASH SITE TODAY

In July of 2014, I threw my mountain bike into the back of my truck and did a day trip up the Suiattle River to check the area out and was pleased to find construction going on to repair the road. I was able to ride my bike eight miles to the Downey Creek Bridge which was still being repaired. From there, I determined, it was another two mile hike to the trail that led up the south side of Sulphur Mountain. A month later I was back with my mountain bike and backpack with provisions to spend two nights.

I had high hopes that the road and bridge repairs would have been completed by now but I was sadly mistaken. Again, I rode my mountain bike the eight miles to the Downey Creek Bridge and found no way to get my bike across the unfinished bridge approach. So, I stashed my bike and hiked the remaining two miles to Sulphur Creek Campground where I set camp for the night.

At 6:00 am the following morning I was heading up the 4 ½ miles of switch back trail that led up the south side of Sulphur Mountain. Somehow I had convinced myself that I would be able to get to the wreck and back out before nightfall. The trail was in terrible condition as it had not been maintained in over eight years. It seemed like every switch back had a large tree fallen over it. It was one obstacle after another.....and no water. It took nearly six hours to reach the top and there I found myself staring down into a deep canyon that had to be crossed before I could access the area where the plane wreck lie. Having only brought supplies for the day, I knew this attempt was already a dismal failure. I ate lunch and took some photos of Sulphur Mountain Lake and the mountain peak above it before retreating back down the switch back trail with my tail between my legs. It was dusk by the time I made it back to my camp. Disgusted with my lack of progress, I became determined to find another route into the crash site.

By the spring of 2015, the road and bridge repairs

had been completed and I was able to drive the whole distance to the foot of Sulphur Mountain. I did a day hike trip up Sulphur Creek to see if it might be possible to access the crash site from this direction and it looked promising. Later that summer, my oldest son, John, joined me as we attempted to follow the stream up the west side of the mountain that drained out of the upper canyon where the plane wreck was. John, now thirty-nine, had shared many adventures with me and had been hiking with me since he was ten. This route turned out to be much better than the switch back trail that climbed up the south side of the mountain and there was an abundance of water. We unfortunately had not given ourselves enough time to reach the top. As we hiked back out we were already making plans for a five day trip the next summer.

August 21st, 2016 was here before we knew it. I had picked up my grandson Tyler Coleman in Olympia the night before, and we arrived back home about midnight. Tyler was a brawny seventeen year old who had done many hiking trips with me in the past. Running on less than four hours sleep, we met John at Arlington at 6:30 am and proceeded up to Sulphur Mountain. John had brought a beautiful laser cut stainless steel plaque that he had special ordered with the names of the three crewmen inscribed on it. I had brought a small drill and stainless fasteners to help mount the plaque.

By 8:30, John, Tyler, and I were starting the hike up Sulphur Creek. The first mile and a half was actually on the old Sulphur Creek Trail that winds up past the Sulphur Warm Springs. The trail is passable up to the mile and a half mark where it ends at an old land slide. The trail is virtually nonexistent beyond this point. About a hundred yards further upstream is a large fallen tree that we used as a foot bridge before continuing up the opposite side of Sulphur Creek. John and I had been up here several weeks earlier marking the route so we could make better time.

At 2:00 we had arrived at the foot of the mountain where the stream tumbles down from the upper canyon that conceals the crash site. After a quick lunch break we decided to proceed up the mountain to a small mountain lake where we could make camp.

The ascent up the side of the mountain with a heavy pack was a bit more difficult than I had anticipated due to the steep slope. Another problem was the ground wasp nests. They were everywhere. We probably walked through a dozen of them and we all ended up getting stung multiple times. Our forward progress slowed considerably and it became obvious that we were not going to make it to the top before dark. The decision was made to find as level a spot as possible and dig in for the night. What a miserable night that was.

The following morning we finished the climb to the top where we found several acres of level ground with a beautiful stream meandering through it. Close by was the small, pristine mountain lake. I was not feeling well at this point. I had overdone it the day before and I hadn't gotten much sleep in two days. At sixty-three years of age, I should have known better. After setting up camp, I lounged for the rest of the day while John and Tyler did some exploring.

On day three, we awoke to a beautiful morning. It was clear and calm as it had been the two previous days. I was feeling better but still didn't have much of an appetite. I forced myself to eat a cup of instant oatmeal as we made plans for the day. Both John and Tyler were well rested and ready to go. Today we planned on locating the crash site, mapping out the debris field, and finding a place to mount the memorial plaque.

John took the lead as we worked our way through a maze of huge boulders and started up into the north entrance of the mountain canyon. According to the information I had compiled, we would find the aircraft at the south end of the canyon. We followed a small stream which passed through a meadow carpeted with mountain heather. I think we were all awestruck with the scenery. It was difficult to imagine the tragedy that had occurred here seventy-one years earlier. As we neared the south end of the canyon, I spotted a reflection about half way up the west canyon wall. John climbed up for a closer look and determined it to be a piece of riveted aluminum. The carpet of mountain heather faded into a large rock slide area as we arrived at the canyon's south end. Strewn over the large boulders was the tangled, smashed debris of an aircraft.

At first it was difficult to identify what we were looking at; seventy plus winters of heavy mountain snow had flattened the wreckage and formed it around the large boulders. After a close examination, we were able to determine that this was the remains of a Douglas C-47. We had indeed found the resting place of Dakota FZ-583.

Above us, on the southwest side of the canyon was an obvious trail of debris. The three of us split up as we climbed up through the scattered aluminum debris taking notes and photographing what we found. The entire aircraft appeared to still be here. The left engine and landing gear were found about a hundred yards above the main section of the wreck. The right engine and landing gear had tumbled around the south rim of the canyon and was about a quarter mile away. We circled around and met back at the main section of wreckage which included the wings, tail, and about half of the shattered fuselage. Strewn over the wreckage were several lengths of rotten rope that were no doubt used by McChord's Sgt. Talbert as he searched for the remains of the three crewmen.

As we probed deeper into the wreck, we started finding shoes and pieces of rotted clothing. We stopped at this point not wanting to disturb anything. After all, this was not only a crash site but a burial site as well. We decided to mount the memorial plaque on the wing root which was still attached to both the wings. John held the plaque in place while I drilled the holes and screwed in the fasteners. After we finished and had a few minutes of silence, we began comparing notes and photos of what we had found in the debris field.

From this we were able to determine that the Dakota crew had been flying on almost a dead east heading when they encountered the mountain on the west side of Sulphur Mountain Lake. Sgt. Sorfleet and P/O Bayston must have seen disaster coming at the last minute and pulled up hard. The aircraft appeared to have nosed up over the peak and broke apart as it dove down the east face striking the top of a large rock outcropping. Death would have most certainly been instantaneous. Still, there is no definite answer to why the crew ended up this far off course. It appears that after rounding the south tip of Vancouver Island, they set a dead east course at approximately 6000 feet of altitude and flew for 113 miles striking the first high mountain they came to. A partial explanation would be the inexperience of all three crewmen. They may have been following the wrong navigational radio beam or just become disoriented and got lost. Whatever the cause, they ended up here and remain here on this mountain slope to this day.

As we began the return trip back to camp we turned for a last look up the canyon. What a truly beautiful place this was. You couldn't ask for a more scenic final resting place. It's just unfortunate that these three RCAF crewmen were so young and still had their lives ahead of them. Our thoughts remained with them as we started the two day trip back to civilization. We spent the last night beside a deep pool on Sulphur Creek at the foot of the mountain. John managed to catch a trout large enough to feed the three of us. It was the best meal of the whole trip. What an adventure this had been and it was sad to see it coming to an end. I never could have done it without the help of John and Tyler. We had helped bring closure to three families across the globe and in the process, provided ourselves with an adventure we would remember for the rest of our lives.

An RCAF Douglas C-47 Dakota very similar to FZ-583. (Cye Laramie Collection)

Daniel Victor Sorfleet in his RCAF uniform. The white fabric on his cap indicates he was in training. (Photo courtesy of Ally Ellis)

Back Row 2nd from left; P/O John Charles Eric Bayston, 5th from left; Sgt Charles Arthur John Wilton, after completing training at Comox in May, 1945. (Cye Laramie Collection)

John Laramie searching for a path through boulders blocking the north entrance of the upper canyon. This would be the last obstacle in our quest of finding the C-47 wreck. (Photo by Cye Laramie)

The tail section of the Dakota still shows signs of camouflage paint. (Photo by Cye Laramie)

Cargo door lying beside rear fuselage that has been flattened by 70+ years of heavy snowfall. (Photo by Cye Laramie)

A section of the crushed forward fuselage. (Photo by Cye Laramie)

The emergency radio transmitter nicknamed a "Mae West" because of its unusual waistline shape was found in the debris field. (Photo by Cye Laramie)

Left overhead control panel from the cockpit has the word "master" etched above one of the switches. This was most likely by a young pilot trying to familiarize himself with the aircraft. (Photo by Cye Laramie)

The left engine was found on the slope about 100 yards above the main section of wreckage. (Photo by Cye Laramie)

The left landing gear was found just above the left engine. (Photo by Cye Laramie)

The right engine had tumbled over a quarter of a mile before coming to rest. (Photo by Cye Laramie)

This propeller blade was found perched in the rocks near the right engine. (Photo by Tyler Coleman)

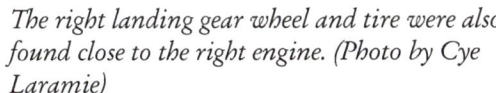

The right landing gear wheel and tire were also found close to the right engine. (Photo by Cye Laramie)

Left to right; John, Cye, and Tyler pose for a photo after mounting the memorial plaque between the wings. (Photo by Cye Laramie)

A close up of the memorial plaque. (Photo by Cye Laramie)

Chapter 28

In Weather Over Mountains And Out Of Gas

By David L. McCurry

RESIDENTS living around the general vicinity of Challis, Idaho, were aroused by the sounds of aircraft engines as they witnessed a bomber circling overhead at approximately 3,000 feet above the surface on March 30, 1943. Shortly before 10:00 pm on this night, many described what they saw as a steady light or possibly the bomber being on fire. After as many as five circling turns to the right, the bomber then headed off in a southeasterly direction.

Raymond Rogers, a rancher located six miles southeast of Challis, reported that he thought the steady light might have been a flare which appeared to light up the side of a mountain in the area. As the bomber headed off on a southeasterly direction the sounds of the engines stopped and then a red-orange fire could be seen in the mountains for an hour after it had crashed.

M.H. Shull, the sheriff of Custer County, Idaho, was in Challis the night of March 30, 1943 and witnessed the bomber circling and then heading in a southeast direction. Thinking that the plane was attempting a landing, he rounded up some cars and drove out to the local airport to light up the runway. After seeing the bomber make one more turn, it then proceeded on a heading to the southeast. A few minutes later several men came running toward him and stated that they believed the bomber had crashed. A very distinct orange glow could then be seen on the mountainside.

Sheriff Shull rounded up a few more men and organized a search party. The group trekked all night long over rough terrain and snow finally arriving at the scene located twenty-two miles southeast of Challis at 11:30 am on the morning of March 31st. They were guided to the crashed bomber by smoking timber surrounding the site. Shull and two others searched around the left wing and other parts of wreckage from the plane looking for any signs of human remains, and found nothing. Lieutenant Sidney Schleimer along with a search party from the Pocatello Army Air Base, Idaho, arrived at approximately twelve o'clock pm and assisted in searching for bodies in which none were found.

The accident aircraft, Boeing B-17F, serial number 42-29514, with a nine member crew aboard which consisted of 2nd Lt. Joseph R. Brensinger (pilot); F/O Harold E. Thompson (co-pilot); 2nd Lt. Austin Finley (navigator); 2nd Lt. George W. Smith (bombardier); S/Sgt. Henry G. Van Slager (engineer); S/Sgt. Howard A. Pope (assistant engineer); S/Sgt. Morris Becker (radio operator); S/Sgt. Harvey R. Wiegand (assistant radio operator); and S/Sgt. Erwin W. Grundman (gunner), first took off at 1300 Pacific War Time (PWT) from the Walla Walla Army Air Field, Washington, with instructor navigator Lt. Bigelow aboard to calibrate their compass and airspeed instruments. The navigator's compass had been removed so they went to the calibration range to calibrate the airspeed instrument. After the calibration tests were completed, the B-17 then landed back at Walla Walla to drop Lt. Bigelow off at the Army Air Field.

The crew attached to the 2nd Air Force, 88th bomb group, and based at the Walla Walla AAFB then took off again at 1500 (PWT) for some local flying. Pilot, Lieutenant Brensinger, stated that they entered thick clouds and climbed to 15,000 feet flying basic instruments and did not break out of the overcast. He then tried flying the compass with no success. He knew they were close to the field but not sure just where.

When they did not break through the overcast, Lt. Brensinger descended down to within 2,000 feet above the surface of the terrain that he thought they were over, and could not see the ground. Lt. Brensinger then turned the compass set to the Walla Walla navigational radio beam, climbed to 8,000 feet, and started to make an instrument approach. The radio static became so intense that they could not hear the beam signals and then couldn't use the radio compass because the needle would keep spinning. Brensinger then instructed the radio man to contact the ground station in Walla Walla and inform them that they were lost.

Lt. Finley, the navigator, tuned the radio in on the Walla Walla Radio Range beam but could only receive static. Lt. Finley was also trying to pick up other stations on the radio to get a fix and determine their position. At this time they had climbed to 10,000 feet and started picking up ice on the plane.

Without knowing their exact position, they flew a

course that should take them from Walla Walla to Boise, Idaho. Still trying to get a bearing, Lt. Finley was unable to pick up any stations.

Lt. Brensinger asked the assistant engineer, S/Sgt. Howard Pope, along with engineer Sgt. Henry Van Slager, to transfer gas from the bomb bay tank to the wing tanks and then asked the radio man, Sgt. Morris Becker, to notify the ground station informing them that the flight could not pick up the beam. For some reason Brensinger could not contact the Walla Walla tower on the command set. Sgt. Pope then reported back that the bomb bay tank was empty although it was written on Form No. 1 as being full. After several gas transfer checks were made, it was confirmed that the bomb bay tank was empty.

The radio operator was then asked to notify the ground station that they had approximately 350 gallons of gas left, and could probably make it to Gowen Field in Boise, Idaho. The ground station gave them a go ahead so Lt. Brensinger climbed to 14,000 feet; dropped rpm to 1500, manifold pressure to 23 inches, and was still able to hold altitude with a 130 mph air speed. They were still receiving some carburetor and wing ice, but not to serious. They used inter-coolers, deicers, and also some pitot heat.

On a magnetic heading of 132 degrees toward Boise, the B-17 bomber broke out of the clouds at 1900 for about twenty-five minutes and the crew could see the mountains directly below them. Ahead of them were broken clouds and an overcast 2,000 feet above them at 16,000 feet. Lt. Finley tuned in the Boise beam and found them to be on the northeast leg. The crew then reported everything okay and gave their position to the Walla Walla Air Base.

About fifteen minutes later the crew of 42-29514 encountered a large snow storm and again everything closed in around them. While holding a magnetic heading of 205 degrees at 1930, the airspeed indicator went out and the red light on the emergency hydraulic system went on, and then the beam again had cut completely out. All of this flying had also been done with no oxygen on board.

Finally knowing that they could not receive the beam and having only a few minutes of gas supply left; Lt. Brensinger turned the Automatic Flight Control Equipment (A.F.C.E.) gyros on and gave the order to bail out. Brensinger had F/O Harold Thompson make sure everyone had left the plane and then gave orders for Thompson to bail out. Lt. Brensinger set the A.F.C.E. to hold the plane straight, and then went out the navigator's hatch. Time was 2030.

First to jump was assistant engineer Howard Pope followed by the other eight crew members. They had all bailed out over the middle fork of the Salmon River approximately fifty miles northwest of Challis, Idaho.

Lt. Finley landed on the side of a mountain in snow about four feet deep and couldn't move around in the dark, so he stayed where he had landed. He started hollering for a long time and never received an answer. The following morning Lt. Finley hiked down the mountain and found himself on the edge of the Salmon River. The snow was so deep that the only way he could make any forward progress was to wade along the edge of the river. Just before dark that night, he met up with Harold Thompson who was coming down on the other side of the river. They found a small cabin that night but were unable to make a fire to dry them out and keep warm. The two then spent the next day hiking down the river and slept in another cabin that night. The following morning they found their way to a ranger station supplied with food.

After landing and getting out of his parachute, Sgt. Wiegand noticed that he had landed about twenty feet from the edge of the middle fork of the Salmon River. After walking downstream for a short distance, Wiegand started looking for a place to bed down for the night. After lying down for thirty minutes, he then heard someone yell. After yelling back, he found that Sgt. Becker and Sgt. Grundman were proceeding toward him. The three of them then bedded down under a large pine tree until dawn. Grundman had dragged his chute along with him and they used it for cover as best as they could. The next day they waded along the river bank, but at times were forced to crawl through waist deep snow because of the water being too deep. That afternoon Wiegand sighted a small shack on the other side of the river and thinking there might be food in it, removed his heavy jacket and proceeded to wade across the river. Wading in waist deep water; Wiegand lost his balance in the swift current and got completely wet. He grabbed hold of some exposed rocks to keep from being swept away and pulled himself across the river by holding onto the rocks. After crawling 150 yards to the shack, Wiegand tried to make a fire to warm up but found that the lighter he had with him was all wet and would not work. Realizing that he was in a terrible situation, Wiegand called to Becker and Grundman whom waded across the river without mishap bringing his jacket with them. Inside of the shack Grundman had found a few matches and started a fire in the fireplace. After getting himself warmed up, the three men took stock of the place and discovered some musty flour, baking powder, and some grease and sugar that had been rained on. Wiegand mixed what was there and made three small pancakes.

After spending the night in the shack, they found a hammer, axe, and nails on the following morning and built a raft. However the raft would only float one man so they abandoned that idea and set out again downstream. That night they slept on a small cliff overlooking the river and had a fire. The next day they continued down the river and by late afternoon heard a hello, and were then reunited with their navigator, Lt. Finley. Finley led the group to a ranger cabin where they stayed until their rescue. They had plenty of food except bread and shared the cooking. Thus far, eight of the crew members had been rescued without injury.

Aerial searches for the remaining crew member, Sgt. Van Slager, was conducted and then abandoned after eighteen days during which time no trace of him could be found. Two aircraft which were participating in the search for survivors also crashed in the mountains. To this day, no trace of Sgt. Van Slager has ever been found, and it was thought that either his parachute did not open, or he drowned in the river.

B-17F SERIAL NUMBER 42-29514 CRASH SITE TODAY

Today, southeast of Challis, Idaho, in the Lost River Mountain Range, rests the wreck of Boeing B-17F, serial number 42-29514. A former resident of Challis recovered the nose section and two propellers from the bomber, and the engines, wings, and tail section had also been removed from the plane years ago.

Marc McDonald recently hiked to the crash site and found that there is still quite a bit of scattered items at the site. The two main landing gears were located along with some cockpit items, dummy bombs, and other items from the bomb bay. Along a line of debris scattered one-half mile long; Marc also found two turbochargers and lots of scattered fuselage parts. Like so many other World War II wrecks, it is always intriguing to see this part of our aviation history locked in time.

A Boeing B-17F seen leaving contrails high in the sky closely resembled the B-17F which crashed near Challis, Idaho, on March 30, 1943. (U.S. Army Air Forces)

Marc McDonald examines a turbocharger from B-17F serial number 42-29514. (Photo by Eric Hansen)

Two main landing gears still remain at the crash site. (Photo by Marc McDonald)

Stenciled writing on wreckage from the B-17 bomber was still very legible after 70+ years sitting on the mountain. (Photo by Marc McDonald)

Parts of many practice bombs were seen at the site. (Photo by Marc McDonald)

A toothed ring from the base of a gun turret. (Photo by Marc McDonald)

Armor plating was also found at the site. (Photo by Marc McDonald)

Bomb release solenoid from the plane's bomb bay. (Photo by Marc McDonald)

Pilot's seat adjustment rails looked like they were shiny new. (Photo by Marc McDonald)

Trail of wreckage from 42-29514 extended one-half mile up the mountain. (Photo by Marc McDonald)

Large piece of the B-17's fuselage still remaining at the crash site. (Photo by Marc McDonald)

An oxygen bottle from the bomber with an exhaust pipe stuck in the middle of it. (Photo by Marc McDonald)

A major piece of the wing structure from B-17 s/n 42-29514 still remaining at the crash site. (Photo by Marc McDonald)

Appendix I

Washington State Crash Locator List

Type of Aircraft	Identification	Date of Crash	Location
TBM	Unknown	Approx. 1940	4702N 12350W
B-18A	37-523	16 Jan 1941	4639N 12222W
B-24	4443	16 Jun 1941	4737N 11700W
B-25	Unknown	12 Sep 1941	4746N 12307W
B-17E	41-2598	15 Jul 1942	4600N 11811W
B-24D	41-23648	16 Jul 1942	4737N 11700W
P-38	Unknown	02 Aug 1942	4825N 12207W
B-17G	42-5367	11 Feb 1943	4601N 11755W
B-17F	42-29500	29 Mar 1943	4702N 12011W
B-17F	42-5313	29 Mar 1943	4719N 11920W
B-25D	41-29836	10 May 1943	4718N 11802W
P-38E	41-2052	12 May 1943	4755N 12306W
PV-1	33142	14 May 1943	4733N 12313W
B-17F	42-2998	21 Jun 1943	4651N 11950W
B-17F	42-5289	10 Aug 1943	4551N 11951W
NE-1	26260	10 Aug 1943	4822N 12219W
R5D-6	39361	11 Aug 1943	4830N 12100W
FM-1	15269	23 Oct 1943	4723N 12313W
P-38H	42-66778	10 Nov 1943	4704N 12007W
P-39	4138253	09 Dec 1943	4808N 12152W
JRF	Unknown	1943	4302N 12357W
F6F	Unknown	1943	4801N 12154W
F4F	03426	23 Jan 1944	4625N 12313W
F4F	05077	23 Jan 1944	4626N 12313W
TBF	06090	24 May 1944	4759N 12313W
A-24	Unknown	18 Apr 1944	4639N 12152W
P-39D	41-7009	02 May 1944	4718N 11929W
P-39K	42-4394	27 May 1944	4729N 11928W
FM-2	55071/55225	Jun 1944	15 mi SW Pasco
P-39Q	44-2269	29 Jun 1944	4717N 11931W
BT-13	42-90677	04 Jul 1944	4724N 11956W
P-39Q	44-2426	04 Jul 1944	4657N 11919W
P-39Q	42-20800	10 Jul 1944	4802N 11902W
P-39Q	44-2328	18 Jul 1944	4721N 11845W
B-24J	42-51617	19 Jul 1944	4607N 11838W
P-39Q	42-19719	22 Jul 1944	4654N 11945W
P-39Q	42-20020	31 Jul 1944	4652N 11928W
P-39Q	42-19715	02 Aug 1944	4651N 11927W
P-63A	42-69016	09 Aug 1944	4800N 11902W
P-39Q	42-20857	09 Aug 1944	4733N 11929W
P-39	42-8876	09 Aug 1944	4733N 11928W
P-39Q	42-20012	09 Aug 1944	4737N 11923W
P-39Q	44-2373	11 Aug 1944	4653N 11942W
P-39Q	44-2281	17 Aug 1944	4653N 11942W
F6F-3	42889	09 Sep 1944	4625N 11855W
P-38L	44-24338	27 Sep 1944	4712N 11915W
B-24J	42-78579	29 Sep 1944	4718N 12026W
P-38L	44-23914	30 Sep 1944	4646N 11917W
P-38L	44-24827	06 Oct 1944	4721N 11932W

Type of Aircraft	Identification	Date of Crash	Location
F6F	42751	13 Nov 1944	4604N 11756W
PV-1	Unknown	1944	4757N 12313W
Unknown	Unknown	1944	4801N 12314W
PV-1	33380	14 Jan 1945	4820N 12105W
FM-2	47092	08 Feb 1945	4807N 12133W
JM-1	66654	14 Feb 1945	4817N 12206W
SBD	36638	15 Feb 1945	4725N 12116W
C-47	Unknown	04 Apr 1945	4724N 12112W
B-24J	42-64156	15 Jun 1945	4607N 11838W
PBY	Unknown	02 Aug 1945	4800N 12311W
PT-22	NC49393	03 Sep 1945	4618N 12203W
TBM	53215	12 Oct 1945	4536N 12150W
B-24	42-64160	01 Nov 1945	4619N 12310W
B-24	42-73191	01 Nov 1945	4720N 12211W
PV-1	N49459	29 Nov 1945	4610N 12200W
PB4Y	Unknown	Nov 1945	4803N 12201W
F4U	81109	27 Dec 1945	4600N 12226W
F4U	81527	27 Dec 1945	4626N 12116W
BT-13	NC49307	10 Apr 1946	4735N 11749W
UC-78	NC49280	26 Apr 1946	4717N 12123W
RA-24B	42-54295	27 May 1946	4636N 12009W
PBY-6A	63999	16 Sep 1946	4812N 12153W
AT-6	NC49310	31 Oct 1946	4757N 11705W
R5D	39528	10 Dec 1946	4652N 12147W
PT-22	NC57167	25 Jun 1947	4618N 12033W
PB4Y2	59821	22 Jul 1947	4820N 12237W
B-25	44-31316	01 Aug 1947	4608N 12244W
PT-23	NC9429	03 Aug 1947	4713N 11805W
B-29	9989	04 Nov 1947	4723N 11842W
B-29	44-62063	13 Nov 1947	4754N 11706W
PT-19	NC49428	21 Dec 1947	4659N 12000W
PT-23	Unknown	1947	4629N 12101W
BT-13	NC49282	1947	4622N 12308W
T-6	41-32385	04 Feb 1948	4857N 12217W
C-47	AF6267	21 Mar 1948	4601N 12235W
T-11	AF9496	02 Apr 1948	4803N 12147W
A-26	41-39526	09 Apr 1948	4611N 12237W
BT-13	58833	17 Apr 1948	4630N 12131W
F6F	78111	19 Oct 1948	4748N 12202W
BT-13	NC3032	30 Nov 1948	4711N 12155W
C-47	AF5931	07 Jan 1949	4644N 12210W
C-82	AF8582	29 Sep 1949	4705N 12311W
G-54	AF2474	22 Nov 1949	4611N 12210W
PT-19	51331	14 May 1950	2 mi W Cashmere
Stearman	NC61326	27 Jun 1950	4558N 12109W
Stearman	N58312	06 Jul 1950	4602N 11807W
PT-23	Unknown	29 Aug 1950	4814N 11925W
Martin 202	N93054	16 Jan 1951	4732N 11758W
C-47	9266	11 Mar 1951	4755N 11704W
SB-17	44-85746	19 Jan 1952	4751N 12305W
BT-13	NC8565	19 Jan 1952	4559N 11737W
F-89	5797	Aug 1952	4812N 12230W
C-124	50-100A	20 Dec 1952	4713N 11918W
DC-4	N574	07 Jan 1953	4730N 12202W
PB-Y2	59937	28 Jan 1953	4748N 12126W
T-11	AF7572	12 Apr 1953	4549N 12143W

Type of Aircraft	Identification	Date of Crash	Location
DC-3	NC65743	14 Apr 1953	4726N 12127W
C-46	NC1693	23 Apr 1953	4722N 12144W
C-97	N1390	24 Mar 1953	4650N 12250W
F-94	4646	12 Aug 1953	4752N 12251W
F-86	2588	12 Aug 1953	4752N 12251W
DC-3	N19941	01 Sep 1953	4643N 12236W
C-46	N574	01 Jul 1953	Unknown
SNJ-2	N5600V	05 Dec 1953	4751N 12121W
T-33	AF516913	28 Dec 1953	4720N 12245W
F-86	AF518404	19 Mar 1954	4854N 11840W
F-86	3643	09 Aug 1954	4725N 12323W
F-86	8376	09 Aug 1954	4728N 12323W
F-86	AF956	22 Mar 1955	4707N 12155W
F-86D	515956	22 Mar 1955	4716N 12205W
PT-26	N1036N	Mar 1955	4710N 12119W
F-86D	53-958	27 Jun 1955	4657N 11909W
F-86D	52-10081	12 Dec 1955	4728N 11858W
F-89	AF53-2841	02 Mar 1956	4716N 12140W
F-89	AF53-2847	02 Mar 1956	4716N 12140W
F-89	54-313	04 Oct 1956	4747N 12337W
F-89	54-293	04 Oct 1956	4748N 12334W
F-94	Unknown	Dec 1956	4601N 12130W
DC-4	Unknown	Unknown	4830N 12100W
DC-4	N90449	02 Mar 1957	4759N 12251W
RF-84K	52-7278	15 Mar 1957	4741N 11715W
L20A	N532806	12 Jan 1959	4833N 12042W
F-104A	56-783	13 Feb 1959	4756N 11905W
T-33	529703	26 May 1961	4755N 12424W
P2V	331A	22 Mar 1962	4610N 12220W
KC-135A	60-352	10 Sep 1962	4756N 11708W
F-102	AF-561344	08 Feb 1964	4744N 12324W
F-102	Unknown	02 Aug 1964	4718N 11916W
DC-6	N6541C	23 Apr 1965	4651N 12148W
KC-135A	56-3613	19 Jan 1967	4753N 11703W
T-33	Unknown	16 Apr 1968	4659N 12144W
CV-880	JA8028	24 Jun 1969	4712N 11919W
F-102A	Unknown	Unknown	4704N 12331W

Appendix II

Oregon Crash Locator List

Type of Aircraft	Identification	Date of Crash	Location
B-18A	39-26	03 Feb 1942	4419N 11943W
B-25	Unknown	1942	4545N 11807W
B-17E	41-2559	15 Mar 1942	4519N 11852W
A-29	41-23446	03 May 1942	4439N 11737W
B-17E	41-2598	17 Jul 1942	4600N 11811W
P-38F	41-2326	08 Nov 1942	4515N 11854W
P-38F	41-2300	08 Nov 1942	4515N 11854W
B-17F	42-30326	02 Aug 1943	4520N 12359W
B-17F	42-3503	10 Aug 1943	4545N 11949W
B-17F	42-30655	16 Aug 1943	4541N 11807W
B-17	Unknown	Unknown	4557N 11745W
C-45	Unknown	14 Sep 1944	4529N 11823W
F6F-3	42815	13 Oct 1944	4407N 11924W
B-24J	42-50559	16 Oct 1944	4512N 11910W
P-38L	44-24838	09 Feb 1945	4306N 12022W
B-24D	42-63895	12 Feb 1945	4555N 11738W
B-24J	42-50564	25 Aug 1945	4543N 11800W
TBM	Unknown	Unknown	4536N 12150W
TBM-3	53215	19 Oct 1945	4455N 11854W
T-11	37328	11 Dec 1945	4525N 12035W
P-51	4431	14 Feb 1946	4525N 12246W
BT-13	NC58635	21 Dec 1946	4533N 12223W
BT-13	NC64673	09 Jun 1947	4543N 11801W
PT-19	NC49416	1948	4531N 12204W
B-26	N9426F	21 Apr 1949	4522N 12146W
Lancaster Mk.10MR	KB995	26 May 1953	4241N 12408W
B-52D	56591	23 June 1959	4340N 11943W
F-89	54284	22 Oct 1959	4526N 12135W
F-89	532581	25 Feb 1961	4541N 12255W
F-102	57-0896	07 Feb 1963	4509N 12351W
F-101	Unknown	06 Apr 1965	4324N 12055W
DC-9	N9101	02 Oct 1966	4515N 12158W
F-27	N2712	10 Mar 1967	4207N 12139W
A-6	155721	19 Sep 1973	4306N 12022W
A-6	155634	29 May 1973	4320N 12237W
DC-7	N4SW	14 Sep 1979	4213N 12211W
EA-6B	NH-500	03 Mar 2006	4556N 11849W

Appendix III

Idaho Crash Locator List

Type of Aircraft	Identification	Date of Crash	Location
Lockheed 10-A	NC14935	18 Dec 1936	4723N 11603W
B-24	4443	16 Jun 1941	4737N 11700W
B-23	39-052	29 Jan 1943	4509N 11550W
B-17F	42-29514	30 Mar 1943	4430N 11512W
C-43	Unknown	05 Apr 1943	4430N 11510W
B-24J	42-100050	09 Feb 1945	4218N 11339W
P-38	Unknown	11 Mar 1945	4325N 11535W
C-165	C19448	26 May 1945	4450N 11531W
BT-13	NC325	21 Feb 1946	4324N 11553W
BT-13	NC56962	29 Apr 1947	4741N 11629W
C-47	Unknown	01 Jan 1958	4445N 11648W
T-33	17419	06 Sep 1962	4317N 11432W
B-17F	42-29563	02 Dec 1943	4700N 11639W
B-47E	52-0553	23 Aug 1962	4412N 11603W
TBM	Unknown	Unknown	4537N 11353W
T-6	Unknown	Dec 1963	4313N 11528W
C-45	277	09 Jul 1965	4450N 11450W
F4D	65889	04 Oct 1969	4223N 11603W
RF-4C	65-0860	12 Nov 1970	4208N 11358W
RF-4C	Unknown	1975	4330N 11545W
C-130	62-1838	13 May 1995	4306N 11457W

Bibliography and Suggested Reading

Alexander, Sigmund Col. *B-47 Aircraft Losses*. Spiral bound and available direct from the author (12110 Los Cerdos St., San Antonio, TX 78233-5953); Newspaper clippings, reports, and photos of all B-47 losses.

Andrade, John M. *U.S. Military Aircraft Designations and Serials Since 1909*. Hinckley, Leics, Endland. Midland Counties Publications, 1979.

Bailey, Dan E. *World War II Wrecks of the Truk Lagoon*. Redding, California. North Valley Diver Publications. 2000.

_____. *WWII Wrecks of the Kwajalein and Truk Lagoons*. Redding, California. North Valley Diver Publications. 1989.

_____. *World War II Wrecks of Palau*. Redding, California. North Valley Diver Publications. 1991.

Bartelski, Jan. *Disasters in the Air: Mysterious Air Disasters Explained*. London. Airlife Publishing, Ltd. 2001.

Bradley, E. Philip with Richard F. Gaya Sr. *The Crash of Piedmont Flight 349 into Bucks Elbow Mt. as told by the Sole Survivor, E. Philip Bradley*. Available direct from the author: Philip Bradley, P.O. Box 3219, Monroe, NC 28111-3219

Brandt, Trey. *Faded Contrails: Last Flights Over Arizona*. Phoenix, Ariz. Acacia Publishers, 2003.

Cass, William F. *The Last Flight of Liberator 41-1133: The Lives, Times, Training and the Loss of the Bomber Crew Which Crashed on Trail Peak at Philmont Scout Ranch*. West Chester, Pennsylvania. The Winds Aloft Press. 1996.

Cole, Ben. *Four Down on Old Peachtree Road*. Suwanee, Georgia. Crosswind Publications, Ltd. 2007.

Darby, Charles. *Pacific Aircraft Wrecks ... And Where to Find Them*. Melbourne, Australia. Kookaburra Technical Publications Party Ltd., 1979.

Denham, Terry. *World Directory of Airliner Crashes: A Comprehensive Record of more than 10,000 Passenger Aircraft Accidents*. Somerset, England. Patrick Stephens Ltd., 1996.

Field, Andrew J. *Mainliner Denver: The Bombing of Flight 629*. Boulder, Colorado. Johnson Books. 2005.

Hayes, David. *The Lost Squadron: A Fleet of Warplanes Locked in Ice for 50 Years...Can They be Freed to Fly Again?* New York. Hyperion. 1994.

Hoffman, Carl. *Hunting Warbirds: The Obsessive Quest for the Lost Aircraft of World War II*. New York. Ballantine Books. 2001.

Imparato, Edward T. *Into Darkness: A Pilot's Journey Through Headhunter Territory*. Charlottesville, Virginia. Howell Press, Inc. 1995.

Job, Macarthur. *Air Disaster*. Weston Creek, Australia. Aerospace Publications Pty. Ltd. 1994. Volumes One through Four (published in 1995, 1996, 1999, and 2001 respectively).

Kearns, David A. *Where Hell Freezes Over: A Story of Amazing Bravery and Survival*. New York. Thomas Dunne Books (St. Martin's Press). 2005.

Macha, Gary Patric and Don Jordan. *Aircraft Wrecks in the Mountains and Deserts of California* (1909-2002, Third Edition). Lake Forest, CA. InfoNet Publishing, 2002.

Macha, Gary Patric. *Historic Aircraft Wrecks of San Bernardino County*. Charleston, South Carolina. History Press, 2013.

Macha, Gary Patric. *Historic Aircraft Wrecks of Los Angeles County*. Charleston, South Carolina. The History Press, (Nov. 18, 2014.)

Mann, Robert A. *Aircraft Record Cards of the United States Air Force (How to Read the Codes)*. Jefferson, North Carolina. McFarland & Co. Publishers, 2008.

McCurry, David L., Cye Laramie, Dan Thomas Nelson. *Aircraft Wrecks of the Pacific Northwest: Vol. 1*. Bennington, Vermont. Merriam Press, 2013.

McCurry, David L., Cye Laramie, Don Hinton. *Aircraft Wrecks of the Pacific Northwest: Vol. 2*. Bennington, Vermont. Merriam Press, 2014.

Merlin, Peter W. & Moore, Tony. *X-Plane Crashes: Exploring Experimental, Rocket Plane, and Spycraft Incidents, Accidents and Crash Sites*. North Branch, Minnesota. Specialty Press, 2008.

Mireles, Anthony J. *Fatal Army Air Forces Aviation Accidents in the United States, 1941-1945* (three volumes). Jefferson, North Carolina. McFarland & Co. Publishers, 2006.

Page, Gordon. *Warbird Recovery: The Hunt for a Rare WWII Plane in Siberia, Russia*. New York. iUniverse. 2005.

Panas, Jr., John. *Aircraft Mishap Photography: Documenting the Evidence*. Ames, Iowa. Iowa State University Press. 1996.

Ralph, Barry. *The Crash of Little Eva: The Ultimate World War II Survivor Story*. Gretna, Louisiana. Pelican Publishing Co. 2004.

Serling, Robert J. *The Probable Cause... The Truth About Air Travel Today*. Garden City, New York. Doubleday & Co. 1960.

Sheehan, Susan. *A Missing Plane*. New York. G.P. Putnam's Sons. 1986.

Starks, Richard and Miriam Murcutt. *Lost in Tibet: The Untold Story of Five American Airmen, a Doomed Plane, and the Will to Survive*. Guilford, Connecticut. The Lyons Press. 2004.

Stekel, Peter. *Final Flight: The Mystery of a WWII Plane Crash and the Frozen Airmen in the High Sierra*. Berkeley, California. Wilderness Press. 2010.

Sturkey, Marion. *Mid-Air: Accident Reports and Voice Transcripts from Military and Airline Mid-Air Collisions*. Plum Branch, South Carolina. Heritage Press International. 2008.

Van Waarde, Jan. *US Military Aircraft Mishaps 1950-2004*. Schipol, The Netherlands. Scramble/Dutch Aviation Society. 2005.

Veronico, Nicholas A., Ed Davies, A. Kevin Grantham, Robert A. Kropp, Enrico Massagli, Thomas Wm. McGarry, and Walt Wentz. *Wreckchasing: A Guide to Finding Aircraft Crash Sites*, Castro Valley, CA; Pacific Aero Press, 1992.

Veronico, Nicholas A., Ed Davies, Donald B. McComb Jr., and Michael B. McComb. *Wreckchasing 2: Commercial Aircraft Crashes and Crash Sites*. Miami, FL. World Transport Press, 1996.

Veronico, Nicholas A., Ed Davies, A. Kevin Grantham, Robert A. Kropp, Enrico Massagli, Donald B. McComb, Michael B. McComb, Thomas Wm. McGarry, and Walt Wentz. *Wreckchasing 101: A Guide to Finding Aircraft Crash Sites*. Hugo, Minnesota. Stance and Speed, 2011.

Veronico, Nicholas A. *Hidden Warbirds: The Epic Stories of Finding, Recovering, and Rebuilding WWII's Lost Aircraft*. Minneapolis, Minnesota. Zenith Press, 2013.

Veronico, Nicholas A. *Hidden Warbirds II: More Epic Stories of Finding, Recovering, and Rebuilding WWII's Lost Aircraft*. Minneapolis, Minnesota. Zenith Press, (June 1, 2014.)

Widner, Robert. *Aircraft Accidents in Florida: From Pearl Harbor to Hiroshima*. Lulu.com. 2009.

Young, Cindy Lou. *Out of the Fog: Tragedy on Nantucket*. Alton, New Hampshire. Black Lab Publishing, LLC. 2008.

www.ingramcontent.com/pod-product-compliance
Lightning Source LLC
Chambersburg PA
CBHW040908020526
44115CB00028B/5